The Legacy of
Isaiah Berlin

The Legacy of Isaiah Berlin

edited by

MARK LILLA

RONALD DWORKIN

ROBERT SILVERS

with contributions by

AILEEN KELLY

STEVEN LUKES

AVISHAI MARGALIT

THOMAS NAGEL

CHARLES TAYLOR

MICHAEL WALZER

BERNARD WILLIAMS

RICHARD WOLLHEIM

NEW YORK REVIEW BOOKS

New York

THIS IS A NEW YORK REVIEW BOOK

PUBLISHED BY THE NEW YORK REVIEW OF BOOKS

THE LEGACY OF ISAIAH BERLIN

This edition published in 2001
in the United States of America by
The New York Review of Books
1755 Broadway
New York, NY 10019

www.nybooks.com

Library of Congress Cataloging-in-Publication Data
The legacy of Isaiah Berlin / edited by Mark Lilla, Ronald Dworkin, Robert
Silvers; with contributions by Aileen Kelly ... [et al.].
     p.   cm.
     ISBN 0-940322-59-5 (hardcover: alk. paper)
     1. Berlin, Isaiah, Sir — Contributions in political science. 2. Pluralism
(Social sciences) I. Lilla, Mark. II. Dworkin, Ronald William. III. Silvers,
Robert B. IV. Kelly, Aileen
     JC257.B47 L44 2001

                                                          00-010033

ISBN 0-940322-59-5

Printed in the United States of America on acid-free paper.

March 2001

LIST OF CONTRIBUTORS

RONALD DWORKIN is Quain Professor of Jurisprudence at University College, University of London, and Professor of Law and Philosophy at New York University. His books include *Life's Dominion* and *Freedom's Law: The Moral Reading of the Constitution*.

AILEEN KELLY is a fellow of King's College, Cambridge. She is the author of *Toward Another Shore: Russian Thinkers Between Necessity and Chance* and *Views from the Other Shore: Essays on Herzen, Chekhov, and Bakhtin*.

MARK LILLA is Professor of Social Thought at the University of Chicago. He is the author of *G. B. Vico: The Making of an Anti-Modern* and the editor of *New French Thought: Political Philosophy*.

STEVEN LUKES is Professor of Moral Philosophy at the University of Siena and Professor of Sociology at New York University. His books include *Emile Durkheim: His Life and Work* and *The Curious Enlightenment of Professor Caritat: A Comedy of Ideas*.

AVISHAI MARGALIT is Professor of Philosophy at the Hebrew University of Jerusalem. His most recent books are *The Decent Society* and *Views in Review: Politics and Culture in the State of the Jews*.

THOMAS NAGEL is Professor of Philosophy and Law at New York University. His books include *The View from Nowhere* and *The Last Word*.

ROBERT SILVERS is co-editor of *The New York Review of Books*.

CHARLES TAYLOR is Professor of Political Science and Philosophy at McGill University. His books include *Hegel* and *Sources of the Self*.

MICHAEL WALZER is Professor of Social Science at the Institute for Advanced Study in Princeton, New Jersey, and co-editor of *Dissent*. His books include *Spheres of Justice: A Defense of Pluralism and Equality* and *On Toleration*.

BERNARD WILLIAMS is Deutsch Professor of Philosophy at the University of California, Berkeley, and a fellow of All Souls College, Oxford. His books include *Ethics and the Limits of Philosophy* and *Shame and Necessity*.

RICHARD WOLLHEIM is Chairman of the Philosophy Department at the University of California, Berkeley. His books include *Painting as an Art* and *On the Emotions*.

For further information on Isaiah Berlin visit
www.wolfson.ox.ac.uk/berlin/vl/

CONTENTS

INTRODUCTION

ISAIAH BERLIN'S DEATH in 1997, at the age of 88, left his friends and readers with a profound sense of loss. Berlin had an unusual gift for inspiring in others the excitement he felt in reading the work of the philosophers, poets, musicians, and statesmen he admired—though his own admiration was never unmixed. In his vivid essays in the history of ideas and in his biographical sketches, Isaiah Berlin instinctively kept a critical distance between himself and his subjects, an instinct that served him and them equally well. By discovering and exposing the contradictions in a thinker's thought or in a writer's life, by pointing out how a brilliant statesman's vision could be flecked with blind spots and hemmed in by unconscious limitations, Berlin managed to show how deeply the pluralism he defended in morals and politics was rooted in human experience. And in that way he rendered his own esteem more valuable.

In the fall of 1998, the New York Institute for the Humanities convened a conference to mark the first anniversary of Berlin's death. Memorial services had already been held in Oxford, London, Washington, and Jerusalem, but these had celebrated Berlin's personal qualities—his warmth, his intelligence, his deep love of music, his zest for gossip and his genius in conversation. We believed that a different kind of occasion would also be appropriate—one that focused on his intellectual legacy, in a way he would have appreciated, by opening it to public examination and criticism. The Institute therefore invited a small group of scholars and writers who had engaged critically with Berlin's work to New York for two days of discussion and debate. It was a happy and stimulating occasion. Originally we had no plans to publish the proceedings: most conferences are ephemeral events that soon lose their interest. But a number of considerations persuaded us to change our minds: the quality of the papers presented at the conference, the intensity of the debate they provoked, the large audience that attended the event, and the number of requests for transcripts we received, especially after an article on the conference appeared in *The New York Times*. Publication of this volume was made possible through the support of Daniel and Joanna S. Rose and the editorial assistance of Loretta Landi Sorensen, to whom we wish to express our gratitude.

The different sessions of the New York conference all touched on aspects of "pluralism"—moral, ideological, ethnic, and cultural. Berlin took recognition of and tolerance for pluralism to be the liberal values par excellence, and he believed that his analysis of

pluralism was his main contribution to moral and
political thought. It was also the thread connecting his
strictly philosophical work to his otherwise disparate
investigations into the history of ideas and contemporary politics. This volume begins with an examination
of how Berlin's pluralism grew out of a distinction he
saw in intellectual history, between the "hedgehogs"
who develop all-encompassing, unified theories of human
action, historical experience, and political value, and the
"foxes" who see multiplicity everywhere and who fear
zealots who would sacrifice human dignity on the altar
of an idea. Berlin used these classifications to distinguish
and contrast two large streams of modern thought,
one growing out of the French and German Enlighten-
ments, the other growing out of a less well-understood
source he called the "Counter-Enlightenment," a term
he helped to popularize. Aileen Kelly, Mark Lilla, and
Steven Lukes take different views of the character of
these two streams of thought, and of their relation to
modern liberalism.

The second group of papers assesses Berlin's influential philosophical claim that objectively valid—and
indeed compelling—human values necessarily conflict,
so that the satisfaction of one necessarily implies sacrifice of others, a loss that cannot be redeemed. How are
we to understand this claim, and is it sound? Is it part
of the very concepts of liberty and equality, for example, that each of these ideals can be satisfied only at
the cost of the other? Or do the apparent conflicts that
Berlin identified between the two ideals only reflect
misunderstanding or uncertainty about how to identify

and enforce them? If the cardinal values of liberalism do conflict, does it follow that liberalism must fail, or only that it must take care to avoid extravagant and unrealistic programs? These are the subjects of papers by Ronald Dworkin, Bernard Williams, Thomas Nagel, and Charles Taylor, and of the lively debate among them that followed.

The third set of papers is devoted to the question of nationalism, particularly in the context of Zionism and the state of Israel. As Michael Ignatieff has shown in his fine recent biography, *Isaiah Berlin: A Life*, Berlin's intellectual occupation with the question of nationalism was linked to his passionate concern for the fate of Israel and the Jewish people in the twentieth century. Although in his other work he emphasized the pluralistic clash among values and the compromises they impose, on this subject he insisted that the values of liberalism and the reality of modern nationalism might be harmonized, that the sense of decency cultivated by the one might find root in the sense of belonging provided by the other. Robert Silvers, Avishai Margalit, Richard Wollheim, and Michael Walzer here consider the coherence of "liberal nationalism" as a doctrine and as a practical political aspiration.

The themes discussed at the New York conference by no means exhaust the stimulating richness of Isaiah Berlin's writing, nor were they meant to. The conference did not include discussion of many of his most significant intellectual concerns—Romanticism, statesmanship, and Russian literature among them. We expect, however, that this volume will be joined by many others in a continuing examination of the full range of Isaiah Berlin's extraordinary intellectual achievements.

MARK LILLA

RONALD DWORKIN

ROBERT SILVERS

Part I

HEDGEHOGS AND FOXES

AILEEN KELLY

A Revolutionary without Fanaticism

"... the notion of unity in difference, still more that of differences in unity, the tension of the One and the Many, is his obsessive *idée maîtresse.*"

—Isaiah Berlin, "Herder and the Enlightenment"[1]

AS ABRAHAM LINCOLN once said, "We all declare for liberty; but in using the same *word* we do not all mean the same *thing.*"[2] Isaiah Berlin's life's work was to draw out and dissect the many meanings of the concept, and his method was often to approach settled beliefs from unsettling perspectives. Therefore a distinctive feature of his legacy is his insight into what he called the "important if often maddening irregulars of civilization"—those intellectual mavericks who, from the

---

1. Isaiah Berlin, *Vico and Herder* (The Viking Press, 1976), pp. 153–154.

2. Roy P. Basler, editor, *The Collected Works of Abraham Lincoln* (Rutgers University Press, 1953), Vol. VII, p. 301.

eighteenth century onward, made their wild irruption into "the well-ordered procession of sane and rational European thinkers."[3]

Berlin himself is often seen by his critics as just such a figure. His central dichotomy of monists and pluralists, hedgehogs and foxes, has been interpreted as an all-out attack on the values of the Enlightenment, launched from the hostile and distorting perspective of its more eccentric opponents. It has been argued that his reaction against the despotic consequences of historical teleologies rooted in Enlightenment thought led him to identify too closely with the Counter-Enlightenment in the form of Vico, Herder, and Hamann; his sympathy for these irregulars having blinded him to irreconcilable differences between their irrationalism and his own liberal pluralism.[4]

Berlin had such critics in mind when he remarked in the late 1960s on the "astonishing opinions" imputed to him since the publication a decade earlier of his lecture "Two Concepts of Liberty," which defended the notion of negative freedom against the encroachments of teleological doctrines linking liberty to overarching goals. He had been accused, he said, of ultra-individualism, subjectivism, and extreme relativism, and a blanket endorsement of negative as opposed to positive liberty; but he protested that he was doing no such thing, "since

---

3. Isaiah Berlin, *The Magus of the North: J. G. Hamann and the Origins of Modern Irrationalism*, edited by Henry Hardy (London: John Murray, 1993), p. xvi.

4. See for example Mark Lilla, "The Trouble with the Enlightenment," *London Review of Books*, January 6, 1994.

this would itself constitute precisely the kind of intolerant monism against which the entire argument is directed."[5] Yet surprisingly few of Berlin's critics have sought to address this entire argument. Most concentrate instead on specific areas, a method that skews the picture of the whole. For instance, his views on the historical clash between monists and their critics are often discussed on the basis of his studies of three great enemies of the Enlightenment, while no mention is made of a much larger and more disparate group of thinkers who were central to Berlin's reflections on the problem of freedom: the Russian intelligentsia.

In his essay, "The Pursuit of the Ideal," Berlin has written of the early influence on his thought of the moral approach of nineteenth-century Russian novelists and social theorists—their concern with the roots in the human condition of injustice and falsity in human relations. They made him intensely aware, he writes, that the great ideological storms of the twentieth century were not just the outcome of conflicts of impersonal forces: they "began with ideas in people's heads: ideas about what relations between men have been, are, might be, and should be."[6] Hence his belief that in order to understand and be able to act rationally in our dangerous world, it is imperative that we examine with every intellectual resource we have,

5

---

5. Isaiah Berlin, Introduction, *Four Essays on Liberty* (Oxford University Press, 1969), pp. xlv, lviii, n. 1.

6. Isaiah Berlin, "The Pursuit of the Ideal," *The Crooked Timber of Humanity: Chapters in the History of Ideas*, edited by Henry Hardy (Knopf, 1991), p. 1.

the roots, growth, essence, and above all the validity of the goals and motives that guide human action.

As he notes in that essay, Berlin devoted nearly half a century to this ethical project. It is strange therefore that so little attention has been given to his studies of the Russian thinkers who first sparked his interest in the social and political consequences of alternative ways of perceiving the world. The first monograph on his liberalism mentions only one Russian name—Lenin;[7] while John Gray's decision in his book on Berlin's thought not to address what he calls his subject's "important contribution to Russian studies" seems to reflect a common view that, significant though Berlin's essays on Russian themes are, they represent a personal interest in an area peripheral to his main intellectual enterprise.[8]

On the contrary: they were central to it, in two respects.

First, they gave him a way of discussing hedgehogs and foxes that avoided the risk of reductiveness. The Russian thinkers who interested him were influenced by a vast and very varied range of European ideas and movements—including Enlightenment rationalism, Counter-Enlightenment mysticism, Romantic individualism, German idealism, materialism, positivism, and Marxism. As a group they also shared an unparalleled commitment to ideas as integral visions of the world which, once adopted, must be acted out in private and public conduct. Hence their value as a rich source of concrete examples for Berlin's discussion of the motives

---

7. C. J. Galipeau, *Isaiah Berlin's Liberalism* (Oxford: Clarendon Press, 1994).

8. John Gray, *Berlin* (London: Fontana, 1995), p. 2.

and consequences of monist and pluralist approaches to history and human life.

Secondly, Berlin's admiration for the Russian arch-fox, Alexander Herzen, which has no equal in his estimation of Western theorists, helps to answer what are considered the most contentious questions about his own thought: in particular, the coherence of his vision and the relation of his pluralism to his liberalism.

The intrinsic connection between Berlin's major writings on moral and political theory and his essays on Russian themes is reflected in their parallel chronologies. The principal essays that set down the essentials of his pluralism were published between 1949 and 1959 (and subsequently collected in the volume entitled *Four Essays on Liberty*). Nine of his ten essays on Russian thinkers first appeared between 1948 and 1960. (The exception was his later study of Turgenev). His critique of teleological approaches to history in the long essay, "Historical Inevitability," was made in 1953, the same year as the appearance of "The Hedgehog and the Fox," which depicts the struggle between Tolstoy's skeptical realism and his quest for a universal explanatory principle.[9]

---

9. The essays subsequently collected under the title *Four Essays on Liberty* are "Political Ideas in the Twentieth Century" (1949), "Historical Inevitability" (delivered as a lecture in 1953 and published the following year), "Two Concepts of Liberty" (1958), and "John Stuart Mill and the Ends of Life" (1959). Berlin's essays on Russian themes, collected in the volume *Russian Thinkers*, edited by Henry Hardy and Aileen Kelly (London: The Hogarth Press, 1978) are: "Russia and 1848" (1948); "The Hedgehog and the Fox" (1953); "A Remarkable Decade" (four lectures delivered in 1954 and published in 1955–1956); "Herzen and Bakunin on Individual Liberty" (1955); "Russian Populism" (the

8

There are no Romantic heroes or Enlightenment villains in Berlin's portraits of Russian thinkers, which should remind us that (as he himself remarks in his study of Tolstoy) like all over-simple classifications the hedgehog/fox dichotomy, if pressed, becomes ultimately absurd. The human condition is such that we are all hybrids in this respect: we perceive the world and we reason simultaneously by means of universals and particulars. Berlin's essays on liberty treat monistic doctrines as expressions of a deep and probably ineradicable human need to find a unitary pattern in experience: he stipulates only that we should not allow that need to determine our practice. But he stresses equally the disastrous moral and political consequences of extreme particularism and the irrationalist denial of all universal, generically human standards. The excesses of the Enlightenment helped call forth the excesses of its enemies. Both determinism and relativism, he argues, are founded on fallacious, because one-sided, interpretations of experience.[10]

---

introduction to Franco Venturi, *Roots of Revolution* [London: Weidenfeld, 1960]); "Tolstoy and Enlightenment" (a lecture delivered in 1960 and published the following year); and an essay on Turgenev, "Fathers and Children," a lecture delivered in 1970 and published in 1972.

In addition he wrote introductions to an English translation of Herzen's *From the Other Shore* and *The Russian People and Socialism* (London: Weidenfeld, 1956), and to a translation of Herzen's memoirs, *My Past and Thoughts* (London: Chatto and Windus, 1968).

Shorter pieces on Russian subjects, including radio talks and contributions to the journal *Foreign Affairs*, are listed in the editor's introduction to *Russian Thinkers*.

10. See Berlin, *Four Essays*, pp. 106–107, 172.

The Russian thinkers whom Berlin most admired were strangers to this kind of one-sidedness. He shows how, for historical reasons, they shared a pressing concern with the application of moral principles to concrete situations, which made them unusually sensitive to the competing claims of reason and feeling, freedom and equality, the individual and the social whole, and the relation of ends to means. He believed that we have much to learn from both the illusions and the insights that they revealed in the course of their tormented self-questioning and their passionate debates.

Berlin's approach to Russian thought contrasts sharply with the dominant tendency in the 1950s and 1960s to use the study of Russian history as an ideological weapon in the Cold War. Soviet historians exalted the pre-revolutionary radical intelligentsia as enlighteners and precursors of scientific socialism, while Western liberal scholars depicted the same people as fanatical, deluded utopians who prepared the ground for Bolshevik despotism.[11] Steering clear of the preconceptions that led other liberals to present Russian radical thought as a catastrophic deviation from the tradition that produced the great writers, Berlin discerned the same underlying pattern of conflict in Russian thought of all ideological tendencies: a conflict between the thirst for absolutes, for final and irrefutable truths, and an iconoclastic humanism often expressed in devastating

---

11. For a comparison between this approach to Russian thought and Berlin's see chapters 1 and 2 of my book *Toward Another Shore: Russian Thinkers Between Necessity and Chance* (Yale University Press, 1998).

critiques of revered institutions and traditional author-
ities. He located the sources of this tension in Russia's
anomalous position with regard to her European neighbors: in the mid-nineteenth century it was still a huge
backward country, where a despotic regime maintained
a vast and primitive population in semi-medieval conditions of extreme poverty, oppression, and ignorance.
As he observed, a crisis of conscience was bound to
ensue among the tiny number who constituted Russia's
educated elite; and this, combined with the absence of
any practical outlet for their reforming impulses, helps
explain why so many sought consolation in the great
utopian visions of the March of History as preached
by Hegel and, subsequently, Marx, which assured them
that, as dictated by the universal laws of progress, all
nations, including their own, were advancing inex-
orably toward a universal state of ideal harmony. At
the same time, the vast differences between the Russian
system and those of the West undermined their faith
in universal panaceas, impelling them to look more
closely at specific Russian problems, including the
actual condition and needs of the people, for which
neither Western socialism nor liberal parliamentarism
seemed to offer convincing solutions. From this sober
empirical standpoint a succession of thinkers—such as
Herzen, the critic Vissarion Belinsky (who in a famous
volte-face renounced his Hegelian quietism in favor of
a militant humanism), Tolstoy, and the leaders of
Russian revolutionary populism—launched penetrating and prescient critiques of all teleological theories,
both of the right and the left, which attempted to force

individuals into any single mold or to explain present evils as a dialectical premise of future bliss.

Berlin observes that some of their most effective attacks were made through a procedure vividly expressed in Tolstoy's didactic writings, a "habit of asking exaggeratedly simple but fundamental questions" about cardinal issues of principle, which "cut far deeper, in the deliberately... naked form in which he usually presents them than those of more 'balanced' and 'objective' thinkers."[12]

Berlin often quoted one example of this technique: the following account by Herzen of how he interrupted the French socialist Louis Blanc who was orating on the duty to sacrifice oneself for society.

> "Why?" I asked suddenly.
>
> "How do you mean, 'Why?'—but surely the whole purpose and mission of man is the well-being of society?"
>
> "But it will never be attained if everyone makes sacrifices and nobody enjoys himself."
>
> "You are playing with words."
>
> "The muddleheadedness of a barbarian," I replied, laughing.[13]

But Berlin also shows how even those who were most suspicious of revered doctrines and absolutes were often drawn into self-contradiction by their yearning

---

12. Berlin, *Russian Thinkers*, p. 239.

13. Berlin, *Russian Thinkers*, p. 82.

for ultimate solutions to intolerable moral and political conflicts. Tolstoy's denunciations of the absurd reductiveness of all general theories about history or society were driven by the need to find some unitary truth that would resist his destructive attacks. The anarchist Bakunin demolished the pretensions of all systematizers who sought to prescribe and regulate the forms of human society, and warned of the authoritarianism behind Marx's "scientific socialism," but his own Romantic cult of the creative force of the will to destroy had no less sinister implications. Many of those who dismissed the populists' faith in the uncorrupted virtue of the Russian peasant as utopian fantasy subsequently embraced the Marxist fantasy of the saving mission of the proletariat.

The tension between utopianism and skeptical realism in Russian thought is most vividly conveyed in Berlin's essay on the Russian populist movement, which arose in the 1850s and culminated in the assassination of Alexander II, after which it rapidly declined. While its leaders had very dissimilar outlooks, and groups within the movement tended to differ sharply on questions of ends and means, they all shared "one vast apocalyptic assumption: that once the reign of evil—autocracy, exploitation, inequality—is consumed in the fire of the revolution, there will arise naturally and spontaneously out of its ashes a natural, harmonious, just order, needing only the gentle guidance of the enlightened revolutionaries to attain its proper perfection."[14] They believed

---

14. Berlin, *Russian Thinkers*, p. 217.

that the foundations of such an order already existed in
the Russian peasant commune, which they saw as a
cornerstone on which a loose federal structure of self-
governing units of producers and consumers could be
built, thereby avoiding the development of large-scale
industry and the creation of a pauperized proletariat.
While noting that they largely idealized the commune,
Berlin questions whether they were as deluded as is
generally thought in their belief that full-blown capitalism was neither desirable nor inevitable in Russia. He
observes that they criticized (on ethical and humanitar-
ian grounds) such sacred cows of nineteenth-century
liberal and radical theory as centralization and large-
scale industrialization long before such criticism
became common in the West. They were justified in
protesting that there were no *a priori* reasons why
Russia, which had not yet embarked on unrestrained
industrialization, should inevitably follow the West
along this path, with its dehumanizing consequences: it
was not abstract dogma, but moral revulsion against
the brutal cost of that process that made them seek a
social revolution before capitalism became entrenched
in Russia. The populist conspirators of the 1870s are
often cited as the model for Lenin's party of professional revolutionaries, but Berlin argues that their strict
discipline was a necessity imposed on them by the specific situation in tsarist Russia and did not derive from
a belief in hierarchy as a principle desirable in itself.
Most were deeply democratic: faith in individual freedom was fundamental to their outlook, and their most
thoughtful and scrupulous leaders, such as Nikolai

Mikhailovsky and Piotr Lavrov, honestly and painfully confronted such problems as the contradictions inherent in an intellectual elite making a democratic revolution for the masses. Above all, they never invoked historical inevitability to justify what might otherwise have been patently unjust or cruel:

> If violence was the only means to a given end, then there might be circumstances in which it was right to employ it; but this must be justified in each case by the intrinsic moral claim of the end—an increase in happiness, or solidarity, or justice, or peace, or some other universal human value that outweighs the evil of the means—never by the view that it was rational or necessary to march in step with history, ignoring one's scruples and dismissing one's own "subjective" moral principles . . . on the ground that history herself transformed all moral systems and retrospectively justified only those principles which survived and succeeded.[15]

The conflict between the populists' millenarianism and their faith in human freedom was a source of much moral confusion within the movement. Only one Russian thinker—Herzen—made the view that "history has no libretto" the core element of his philosophy, and thereby moved onto wholly new ground.

Herzen's vision of the self and the world, based on

---

15. Berlin, *Russian Thinkers*, p. 231.

a radical rejection of monistic systems, is so close to Berlin's own outlook (he often referred to Herzen in conversation as "my hero") that his exposition of Herzen's thought provides answers to some of the most debated questions about his own pluralism.

Berlin frequently affirmed that Herzen's genius and originality have as yet been poorly understood. At the time that Berlin's first essays on him appeared, he was known principally in the West as the proponent of an obscure variant of early agrarian socialism—an injustice that Berlin urged must be remedied. Herzen was a European thinker of the first importance, as well as "one of the three moral preachers of genius born on [Russian] soil": he grasped, "as very few thinkers have ever done, the crucial distinction between words that are about words, and words that are about persons or things in the real world." Berlin's writings on Herzen all focus on what he regards as his central perception: "that any attempt to explain human conduct in terms of, or to dedicate human beings to the service of, any abstraction, be it ever so noble—justice, progress, nationality—even if preached by impeccable altruists like Mazzini or Louis Blanc or Mill, always leads in the end to victimization and human sacrifice."[16] Herzen devoted his life as a radical journalist to the cause of freedom, but rejected all the theories of rational progress that underpinned the radical optimism of his time. He argued that our empirical experience of the complexity of human lives and relationships, the infinite variety

16. Berlin, *Russian Thinkers*, pp. 83, 209, 193.

Aileen Kelly

and changeability of human needs and aspirations, and the role of chance in life, cannot be reconciled with the belief that history has a libretto and a final destination. There can therefore be no eternal norms and standards: within certain limits (Herzen believed in the existence of what Berlin called a minimum of values, a "human horizon" without which societies could scarcely survive),[17] we create our own morality.

Berlin emphasizes that this view was free from the hyperbole of subsequent theorists of self-creation. Herzen was a sober empiricist who both stressed the emancipating role of reason and science, and took account of the biological and cultural situatedness of human beings and the part played by inheritance and tradition in shaping their values. Berlin credits him with grasping a fact that made him the forerunner of much twentieth-century thought:

> ... that the great traditional problems which perennially agitate men's minds have no general solutions; that all genuine questions are of necessity specific, intelligible only in specific contexts; that general problems, such as "What is the end (or the meaning) of life?," or "What makes all events in nature occur as they do?" or "What is the pattern of human history?" are not answerable in principle, not because they are too difficult for our poor finite intellects, but because the questions themselves are misconceived, because ends,

17. Berlin, *The Crooked Timber of Humanity*, pp. 18, 11.

patterns, meanings, causes, differ with the situation and the outlook and needs of the questioner, and can be correctly and clearly formulated only if these are understood.[18]

Berlin notes that Herzen's contemporaries were nonplussed by his detachment from party and doctrine: the young radicals attacked him for being "too ironical, too skeptical," insufficiently committed to the destruction of the enemy. His thought cannot be located on any political spectrum: it "hits both right and left: against Romantic historians, against Hegel, and to some degree against Kant, against utilitarians and against supermen, against Tolstoy and against the religion of art, against 'scientific' and 'evolutionary' ethics, against all the churches. It is empirical and naturalistic, recognizes values that are absolute for those who hold them, as well as change, and is overawed neither by determinism nor by socialism. And it is very independent."[19]

We find much the same hit-list in Berlin's attempts to distinguish his own pluralism from theories with which it has been confused. His outlook rested ultimately on what he termed a "sense of reality"—the capacity (whose importance was established by Herder) to understand empathetically the "inner feel" of

---

18. Introduction to Alexander Herzen, *From the Other Shore and The Russian People and Socialism*, translated by M. Budberg and R. Wollheim (London: Weidenfeld, 1956), p. xxii.

19. Berlin, *Russian Thinkers*, p. 205; Introduction to Herzen, *From the Other Shore*, pp. xvi–xvii.

historical situations, values, and forms of life that are not one's own: a sense of the unique flavor and potentials of a given situation, which are compounded of the interplay of factors too complex, numerous, and minute to be distilled into laws.[20]

Berlin's notion of empathy is sometimes interpreted as a form of Romantic subjectivism, but its distinctiveness emerges clearly in his discussion of Herzen. He makes what may seem an extravagant claim: that Herzen's "sense of reality, in particular of the need for, and the price of, revolution, is unique in his own, and perhaps in any age." He defines Herzen's greatest gift (reflected in his autobiographical masterpiece *My Past and Thoughts*) as the complexity of his vision: his "untrammeled understanding" of the tensions between individuals and classes, personalities and opinions both in Russia and the West, the degree to which he grasped the causes, nature and justification of conflicting ideals, including those most antipathetic to his own.[21] He could understand and state the case, both emotional and intellectual, for violent revolution, for denouncing liberal constitutionalism, which offered the masses votes when what they craved were the basic material necessities of life; but he understood no less clearly the aesthetic and moral values of his own highly civilized, aristocratic generation.

Berlin sees Herzen's sense of reality reflected in his

---

20. See Isaiah Berlin, *The Sense of Reality: Studies in Ideas and their History* (London: Chatto, 1996), pp. 1–39.

21. Berlin, *Russian Thinkers*, pp. 207–208.

belief that ultimate human goods are irreducibly diverse and often incompatible, even incommensurable
—a view often regarded as the most controversial component of Berlin's liberalism. He writes that Herzen
could be at times utopian enough (particularly in the
hopes he placed on the socialist potential of the Russian
peasant commune), but, unlike his fellow-socialist Bakunin, he faced such genuine political problems as:

19

> the incompatibility of unlimited personal liberty
> with either social equality, or the minimum of
> social organization and authority; the need to sail
> precariously between the Scylla of individualist
> "atomization" and the Charybdis of collectivist
> oppression; the sad disparity and conflict between
> many, equally noble, human ideals; the nonexis-
> tence of "objective," eternal, universal moral and
> political standards, to justify either coercion or
> resistance to it; the mirage of distant ends, and the
> impossibility of doing wholly without them.[22]

Berlin cites Herzen in support of what is perhaps his
own most contentious position: that liberalism cannot
plausibly stake out some privileged place in history
on the ground that it has a universal claim on reason,
or a foundation in human nature. There need be no
stronger ground for defending liberty, Berlin argues,
than the minimalist view that to be free to choose is an

---

22. Berlin, *Russian Thinkers*, p. 105.

inalienable ingredient in what makes humans human. But given that individuals and cultures have frequently chosen values incompatible with political freedom, one cannot assert that liberal forms of life will always provide the optimal framework for human self-creation. One can answer only for one's own culture and for oneself. Berlin dramatized this point with a reference to Herzen's attack on those who justify their defense of liberty by such universal propositions as "Freedom is the essence of man." Echoing an observation of Joseph de Maistre, Herzen remarked that, despite the existence of flying fish, we do not say of fish in general that their essence is to fly, since most fish display no tendencies in that direction. Yet we persist in arguing that the nature of man is to seek freedom, although throughout history the vast majority of the human race has shown a preference for other values, such as material security. "Why should man alone, Herzen asked, be classified in terms of what at most small minorities here or there have ever sought for its own sake, still less actively fought for?" This skeptical reflection, Berlin writes, was uttered by a man whose entire life was dominated by a single passion—the pursuit of liberty, personal and political.[23]

The combination of skepticism and commitment that Berlin saw in Herzen accords perfectly with the position that (borrowing a quotation from Joseph Schumpeter) he described as his own: "To realize the relative validity of one's convictions . . . and yet stand

---

23. Berlin, Introduction, *Four Essays*, pp. lix–lx, n. 1.

for them unflinchingly, is what distinguishes a civilized man from a barbarian."[24] This formulation has been often questioned: if one's (liberal) ideals have no morally privileged status, why defend them unflinchingly? Berlin frequently declared that he was not a relativist, but also that while he believed both in pluralism and liberalism, the two were not logically connected.[25]

That last proposition has been variously interpreted, but I believe that what Berlin meant emerges clearly enough from his exposition of the argument in what he describes as Herzen's "great polemical masterpiece": his political testament *From the Other Shore*.[26] Addressing the objection that the denial of eternal truths and absolute ideals can lead only to a nihilistic skepticism, Herzen responds that the fact that our ideals may die with us should comfort, not distress us, because this means that each historical period has its own complete reality; its goals and aspirations are ends in themselves, not a means to something else.

The quotations that Berlin selects to convey the essence of Herzen's thought read like concentrated expressions of his own views on the nature of freedom. For example: "Why is liberty valuable? Because it is an end in itself, because it is what it is. To bring it as a sacrifice to something else is simply to perform

---

24. Berlin, *Four Essays*, p. 172.

25. See Ramin Jahanbegloo, *Conversations with Isaiah Berlin* (London: Halban, 1992), pp. 107, 44. See also Berlin, *Crooked Timber of Humanity*, pp. 10–11. For a discussion of the objections to Berlin's position, see Gray, *Berlin*, chapter 6.

26. Berlin, *Russian Thinkers*, p. 194.

an act of human sacrifice." People are "confused by categories that are not fitted to catch the flow of life." "If we merely look to the end of the process, the purpose of all life is death." Or (from a passage to which Berlin often returns): "If progress is the goal, for whom are we working? ... Do you truly wish to condemn the human beings alive today to the sad role of caryatids supporting a floor for others some day to dance on ... a goal which is infinitely remote is ... a deception; a goal must be closer—at the very least the laborer's wage, or pleasure in work performed."[27]

"The historical process has no 'culmination.' Human beings have invented this notion only because they cannot face the possibility of an endless conflict."[28] Thus Berlin sums up the central thesis of *From the Other Shore.* He emphasizes that Herzen (unlike Bakunin, with whom his name is often linked) did not shy away from the consequences of his own logic. While he believed passionately that only socialism could redress the great economic injustices of his time and give the masses a decent life, he refused to regard his ideal as the ultimate goal of human progress. Socialism, he predicted, "will develop in all its phases until it reaches its own extremes and absurdities. Then there will burst forth from the titanic breast of the revolting minority a cry of denial. Once more a mortal battle will be joined in which socialism will occupy the place of today's

---

27. Berlin, *Russian Thinkers*, pp. 197, 196.

28. Berlin, *Russian Thinkers*, p. 98.

conservatism, and will be defeated by the coming revolution as yet invisible to us . . . "[29]

23

Berlin remarks on the originality of the vision behind
this prophecy—made in 1850: even thinkers like Marx,
who recognized the historical contingency of ideals, made
an exception for their own. Berlin himself described the
practical implications of a truly consistent historicism
as follows: "if we allow that Great Goods can collide . . .
in short, that one cannot have everything, in principle
as well as in practice—and if human creativity may
depend upon a variety of mutually exclusive choices:
then . . . What and how much must we sacrifice to
what? There is, it seems to me, no clear reply." There is
a minimum of civilized values on which compromise is
not justifiable. But on others collisions can be softened,
claims balanced, compromises reached: so much liberty,
so much equality, and so on. "The best that can be done,
as a general rule, is to maintain a precarious equilibrium
that will prevent the occurrence of desperate situations,
of intolerable choices—that is the first requirement for
a decent society."[30] Compare this with the following
passages from one of his essays on Herzen:

> He knew that his own perpetual plea for more
> individual freedom contained the seeds of social

---

29. Cited in Berlin, *Russian Thinkers*, p. 98. Berlin observes in "Two Concepts of Liberty": "Principles are not less sacred because their duration cannot be guaranteed." *Four Essays*, p. 172.

30. Berlin, "The Pursuit of the Ideal," in *The Crooked Timber of Humanity*,
pp. 17–18.

atomization, that a compromise had to be found between the two great social needs—for organization and for individual freedom—some unstable equilibrium that would preserve a minimal area within which the individual could express himself and not be utterly pulverized . . .

The heart of his thought is the notion that the basic problems are perhaps not soluble at all, that all one can do is to try to solve them, but that there is no guarantee, either in socialist nostrums or in any other human construction, no guarantee that happiness or a rational life can be attained, in private or in public life. This curious combination of idealism and skepticism . . . runs through all his writings.[31]

A similar ambivalence in Berlin's thought has made him the target of attacks from both liberals and the left, who maintain that the broad Enlightenment tradition of rationalist universalism remains the only firm ground of defense against irrationalist creeds that threaten civilized values.[32] Only an absolute, they imply, can defeat another absolute. But those who interpret

---

31. Berlin, *Russian Thinkers*, pp. 200–201.

32. Perry Anderson interprets Berlin's pluralism as a retreat from moral commitment: "England's Isaiah," *London Review of Books*, December 20, 1990. Citing Berlin's work on Vico as among the most influential of contemporary attempts to revive aspects of Counter-Enlightenment thought while retaining certain features of the Enlightenment outlook (such as liberal politics), Mark Lilla argues that such attempts are historically and philosophically naive: these are "two rival traditions, moving in opposite directions, forcing us to

Berlin's defense of compromise as a retreat from moral commitment, rather like the myopic all-encompassing tolerance of some brands of Anglo-Saxon liberalism, are profoundly mistaken. He came from a different culture, which instilled in him a passionate intolerance of the central component of all evil: violence. He would sometimes describe in conversation the point at which he first became conscious of his loathing of violence: when as a child in Petrograd in February 1917 he witnessed from the balcony of his parents' apartment the terror on the face of a tsarist policeman being dragged away by a revolutionary mob.

"The first public obligation," Berlin asserted in his defense of compromise, "is to avoid extremes of suffering." While desperate circumstances may demand drastic action, trade-offs of rules and principles may reduce the suffering of the innocent in specific cases. "The concrete situation is almost everything."[33]

Many of Berlin's English-speaking readers, I believe, insufficiently appreciate the extent to which his attack

---

choose between them.... *Aut-aut*: the modern world offers no third alternative." *G. B. Vico: The Making of an Anti-Modern* (Harvard University Press, 1993), p. 13. Berlin's view of the matter is summed up in the conclusion to his essay, "The Romantic Revolution": the majority of civilized members of Western societies are inescapably heirs to two traditions—our values have been shaped both by the insights of Enlightenment thought and by the Romantic revolt against it. We "shift uneasily from one foot to another," bringing conflicting standards and perspectives to bear on moral and political problems, but this logically unsatisfactory situation has its compensation in a "historically and psychologically enriched capacity for understanding men and societies." *The Sense of Reality*, p. 193.

33. Berlin, *The Crooked Timber of Humanity*, pp. 17–18.

26 on monistic visions of the world was inspired by a deep sense of outrage at the scale of suffering and destruction inflicted throughout history by those who claimed exclusive possession of the truth. Here is the root of his remarkable affinity with Herzen whose fundamental thesis, he wrote, was "the terrible power over human lives of ideological abstractions."[34] It is noteworthy that, like Berlin, Herzen traced his horror of violence inflicted in the name of ideals back to a specific experience—his witnessing of the bloodshed of 1848 on the Paris streets. Berlin remarks that Herzen was a rare kind of revolutionary: a man ready for violent change, never in the name of abstract principles, but only of actual misery and injustice, so extreme that it was not morally permissible to let it persist.

Herzen's stand on violence led the Left to accuse him of insufficient commitment to the cause. His response is summed up in his essays "To an Old Comrade," addressed to Bakunin, where he affirms the absurdity of the primitive faith in absolutes that had led in the past to emancipation by means of the guillotine, enlightenment through the whip. A genuine commitment to freedom, he wrote, implied a continual readiness to seek accommodations between one's ideal and competing values which were equally precious to others. "No! Great revolutions are not achieved by the unleashing of evil passions . . . I do not believe in the seriousness of men who prefer crude force and destruction to

---

34. Berlin, *Russian Thinkers*, p. 193.

development and arriving at settlements. . . . One must open men's eyes, not tear them out." Berlin cites these phrases to convey the flavor of this "magnificent" work, which he pronounces "perhaps the most instructive, prophetic, sober and moving" of essays on the prospects of human freedom written in the nineteenth century.[35]

Berlin sometimes compared Herzen's sense of reality with that of the most famous Russian liberal, the writer Ivan Turgenev, whose novels were deeply concerned with the social and political questions that divided the educated Russians of his day. He emphasizes Turgenev's efforts to do justice to the full complexity of the goals and beliefs of all the warring parties and ideological groupings of his time, including those with which he had least sympathy. He believed in gradualism, detested revolutionary violence and fanaticism, but admired the selfless courage of the radical youth and attempted to act as a conciliator between the opposing factions of mid-nineteenth-century Russian society. It is sometimes argued that it was with Turgenev, "the well-meaning, self-questioning, troubled liberal, witness to the complex truth,"[36] rather than with the radical Herzen, that Berlin ultimately identified. But his comparison of the two men indicates otherwise. Fundamental to the outlook of both, he writes, was the notion of the complexity and insolubility of the central

35. Berlin, *Russian Thinkers*, pp. 299, 113.

36. Berlin, *Russian Thinkers*, p. 302.

problems of human existence and the absurdity of trying to solve them by means of political or sociological
nostrums; but the difference between them was that
in the final analysis Turgenev was a detached, slightly
mocking observer of the competing claims of equally
ultimate but mutually irreconcilable values, "he enjoyed
almost too much his lack of will to believe . . . he saw
life with a peculiar chilliness." Herzen, on the contrary,
"cared far too violently"[37]; a cool detachment from
life's tragedies was alien to his nature.

In contrast to Turgenev, who became increasingly
inclined to a world-weary skepticism, Berlin's hero
preached his gospel of compromise with unremitting
fervor, although he had ever fewer listeners in the polar-
ized society of his time. Undeterred by his increasing
isolation within the radical movement, he remarked in
the essays addressed to Bakunin that in the progressive
circles in which they both moved far more courage was
needed to advocate gradualism than to call for the most
extreme measures. Compare Berlin's ironic postscript to
his own defense of compromise, cited earlier: "A little
dull as a solution, you will say? Not the stuff of which
calls to heroic action by inspired leaders are made?"
Yet (he quotes the philosopher C. I. Lewis): "There is
no *a priori* reason for supposing that the truth, when it
is discovered, will necessarily prove interesting."[38]

It has been argued that the full subversive force of

---

37. Berlin, *Russian Thinkers*, p. 203.

38. Berlin, "The Pursuit of the Ideal," p. 19.

Berlin's value pluralism has yet to be appreciated; that those who attempt to situate his thought within the Western liberal tradition often fail to perceive how radically it challenges the forms of rationalism at the heart of traditional varieties of liberalism—the conviction that all genuine moral and political questions have one right answer, and that fundamental human liberties and rights and the claims of justice are ultimately compatible.[39] I believe that Berlin recognized in Herzen —arguably the most misunderstood and misrepresented of all Russian thinkers—a subversive much in his own mold: a radical humanist who maintained as he did himself, that the ultimate harmony in which all good things coexist is not only unattainable, but conceptually incoherent; that the answer to the perennial search for the meaning of life lies not in the poetic symmetry of some ordered system of principles, but in the messy, imperfect, and unfinished prose of daily existence. Serious scientists and philosophers now do not deny the powerful role of chance and contingency in nature and history, but for many it is a source of pessimism. Berlin, like Herzen, celebrated it as the ground of moral freedom. There is nothing in this summing-up of Herzen's credo (from Berlin's introduction to *My Past and Thoughts*) to which he did not subscribe himself:

> He believed that the ultimate goal of life was life itself; that the day and the hour were ends in

---

39. This is a central theme of John Gray's study of Berlin.

themselves, not a means to another day or another experience. He believed that remote ends were a dream, that faith in them was a fatal illusion; that to sacrifice the present, or the immediate and fore-seeable future to these distant ends must always lead to cruel and futile forms of human sacrifice. He believed that values were not found in an impersonal, objective realm, but were created by human beings, changed with the generations of men, but were nonetheless binding upon those who lived in their light; that suffering was inescapable, and infallible knowledge neither attainable nor needed. He believed in reason, scientific methods, individual action, empirically discovered truths; but he tended to suspect that faith in general for-mulae, laws, prescription in human affairs was an attempt, sometimes catastrophic, always irrational, to escape from the uncertainty and unpredictable variety of life to the false security of our own sym-metrical fantasies.[40]

I conclude with one of Berlin's comments on Herzen which seems peculiarly appropriate to Berlin himself: his particular sense of reality "led not to detachment or quietism—to the tolerant conservatism of a Hume or a Bagehot"—but was allied to a passionate commitment to freedom, "which made him the rarest of characters, a revolutionary without fanaticism."[41]

---

40. Berlin, Introduction to *My Past and Thoughts*, p. xxxvi.

41. Berlin, Introduction to *From the Other Shore*, pp. xxi–xxii.

MARK LILLA

Wolves and Lambs

WHEN WE WERE young, friendship was a relatively simple matter. We had friends or we didn't; someone was a friend or he wasn't. And by and large we didn't care who the friends of our friends might be. We might be jealous of them, but it never occurred to us to disapprove of them. It occurred to our parents, of course, and they suffered our moral pangs for us.

With age, we all learn that our parents were right: that it is indeed wise to judge our friends by the company they keep. It is difficult to justify this practice reasonably, though not hard to explain in Darwinian terms. Given the opacity of human nature, it is probably a healthy instinct to judge whom and what our friends admire. It is one thing to share principles or general views with someone, quite another to agree about the worth of another human being. I think it can be said that no friendship is fully cemented until the two parties have discovered a shared object of affection or disdain.

The books and essays of Isaiah Berlin are invitations to friendship. I don't believe I am alone in feeling this.

Grief at his death was shared by many people who never met the man, yet were charmed enough by his writing to feel that his judgments were theirs, and that in losing him they had lost something of themselves. The reason is not difficult to find. Berlin's essays in the history of ideas are not only *about* liberalism; they are also displays of the liberal temperament that inspire admiration and imitation. For Berlin believed that liberalism is not just a matter of principle and theory; it is an existential matter, a certain way of carrying oneself in the world and in the company of others. Berlin's essays on past thinkers express something profound about the liberal condition at all times, but they do so indirectly, through examples of individuals faced with difficult intellectual and political problems. My suspicion is that his ideas about the liberal life could *only* be expressed through example.

Yet it is precisely the examples Berlin chose to illustrate his own liberalism that give me pause. Like many of his readers, I came upon the obscure writers Berlin wrote about through his own interpretation of them. After reading Berlin I ached to read Vico, Herder, and Hamann because I expected to find in them novel philosophical approaches to the problems of reason, of language, of human culture, and of toleration. I devoured Herzen and Turgenev to learn what it means to maintain one's dignity in the midst of revolution, and I opened Moses Hess in the hopes of discovering a coherent statement of liberal nationalism. And in every one of these cases, I was disappointed. The more I studied these writers, the less they resembled Berlin's portraits of them. With the Counter-Enlightenment philosophers in particular—with Vico, Herder, and Hamann—I found myself in the company of thinkers whose fundamental principles I rejected, and whose instincts seemed hostile to the liberal ones Berlin himself defended. The friend of my friend, it turned out, was not necessarily my friend. Which raised certain questions about my friend.

Isaiah Berlin's distinction between the hedgehog (who knows one thing) and the fox (who knows many) is just one of many overlapping distinctions that appear in his work. They are all "hedgehoggish" distinctions, if you'll permit the term. They divide all thinkers and thoughts into neat oppositions: the Enlightenment is set out against the Counter-Enlightenment; monism against pluralism; positive liberty against negative liberty. On first coming across these distinctions, one is tempted to accuse Berlin of the very Manicheanism he found so appalling in the hedgehog. But the sympathetic reader soon learns that these are not metaphysical distinctions, they are simply pedagogical. They are meant to help illustrate the puzzle Berlin saw at the heart of modern history. The puzzle is this: how did the optimistic and progressive spirit of eighteenth-century Europe give way to the dark and terrifying world of the nineteenth and twentieth centuries? How did the Europe that produced Goethe and Kant, Voltaire and Rousseau, Tolstoy and Chekhov, also produce the *Lager* and the *Gulag*?

In one way or another, this is what all of Berlin's wide-ranging essays are about. But, as with Tolstoy, there is an unacknowledged and unquestioned philosophy of history lurking beneath them. Berlin believed that history—or at least modern history—is driven by ideas; he also knew that modern history gave birth to unprecedented forms of suffering. He therefore presumed that the history of modern thought must bear at least indirect responsibility for the disasters of our time, and that researching that history could help us to establish culpability. He proceeded in a novel way, separating the major modern thinkers into hedgehogs and foxes, monists and pluralists, and the results were surprising. By reading Berlin we discover that the Enlightenment was not simply about establishing the idea of human rights, limited secular government, the rule of law, and empirical science. In Berlin's narrative, the Enlightenment was an extremist movement of hedgehogs, a *Walpurgisnacht* of philosophical monism that foreshadowed the rise of a new race of despots. The real heroes, unsung and now forgotten, were the foxes, those thinkers who preached a gospel of pluralism, toleration, and moderation. It is these figures that Berlin wished to rescue from obscurity so that we might shore up the sagging foundations of liberal society.

As historical narratives go, this is an appealing one —not least because it appeals to our own liberal temperament. It gratifies us to learn that figures once held in esteem—Kant, Diderot, Condorcet—need to be taken down a peg, and that room in the pantheon should be made for underdogs like Vico, Herder, and Hamann. But not all appealing histories are convincing ones, as this one is not. If we let the hedgehogs and foxes speak for themselves, a very different story begins to emerge.

Let us begin with the Enlightenment. Isaiah Berlin professed himself to be, and indeed was, a child of the Enlightenment. A skeptical child, but a child none the less. He believed in the universal need for human dignity and in man's right and capacity to govern himself free from the dictates of tradition and authority. He knew ignorance to be a curse and felt that man's steady conquest of natural dangers made his life generally happier, healthier, and more human. Yet despite sharing this extensive ground with the Enlightenment, Berlin was deeply troubled by the criticisms put forward by its most vocal critics. The most troubling was that the Enlightenment was "monistic." We should remind ourselves of just what Berlin meant by this term. Monism rests on three suppositions, he believed: that all general questions have true answers; that those answers are in principle knowable to man; and that those answers are all compatible with each other.[1] Berlin accepted the assumptions of monism as appropriate for the natural sciences, but accused the Enlightenment of having applied them indiscriminately to society, with disastrous results. There it gave birth to a utopian ideal of social reconstruction exploited by communists and fascists alike, an ideal, as Berlin put it, "for which more human beings have, in our time, sacrificed themselves and others than, perhaps, for any other cause in human history."[2]

---

1. Isaiah Berlin, *The Crooked Timber of Humanity: Chapters in the History of Ideas*, edited by Henry Hardy (Knopf, 1991), p. 209.

2. Berlin, *The Crooked Timber of Humanity*, p. 237.

So although Berlin credited the Enlightenment with fathering modern liberty, he repeatedly laid the charge of monism at its feet, describing it as absolutist, deterministic, inflexible, intolerant, unfeeling, homogenizing, arrogant, and blind. This is indeed a weighty charge. But is it just? I suppose it can be made to stick to peripheral figures like Holbach, Helvétius, and La Mettrie, who were mad scientists every one. But for the main current of the Enlightenment, in Britain and on the continent, monism was definitely the *problem*, not the solution. What provoked the scorn of Locke, Hume, and Kant, and inspired them to seek new foundations for skeptical empirical science, was the monism of medieval scholasticism and the baroque, rationalist edifices of Leibniz and Malebranche. And what about the charge of intolerance? Can it really be said that Mendelssohn's *Jerusalem* or Lessing's *Nathan the Wise* were unfeeling and intolerant works? Do the adjectives "homogenizing" and "arrogant" apply to Montesquieu's *Spirit of the Laws* or Voltaire's *Philosophy of History*—the latter of which, we recall, begins in China, not in Palestine or Europe? And what about Voltaire's despairing cry, uttered in his poem on the Lisbon earthquake: "*Il faut l'avouer: le mal est sur la terre*"? Can such deep pessimism have inspired others to sacrifice themselves on the altar of utopia and progress? The answer to each and every one of these questions is "no."

When challenged with these examples, Berlin's response was that he had been misunderstood. He never meant to cast a shadow on the Enlightenment's intentions, nor to suggest that we have nothing to learn from its leaders and their books. Rather, he hoped to point out the disturbing political developments that he saw dormant in certain Enlightenment principles, and to draw our attention to their critics, who in many ways proved prophetic. One example is Hamann, a forerunner of modern irrationalism who was a personal friend but philosophical enemy of Immanuel Kant. Berlin thought Hamann had deep insight into the arbitrary nature of philosophical analysis, its ignorance of lived experience, its hostility to creativity, and its unfounded confidence in the human capacity to unmake and remake the world. Other Counter-Enlightenment thinkers had a highly developed sense of social complexity that the Enlightenment lacked and that liberalism needs. From Vico and Herder, for example, we learn that man makes his own nature in history, through language and national culture; that these cultures are indivisible wholes; that the truths they embody can only be imperfectly understood by those outside the culture; and that cultural variety is both inevitable and preferable to cultural uniformity.

Whenever Isaiah Berlin wrote about the Counter-Enlightenment, he was always at pains to insist that he was separating the useful grain of their thought from the senseless chaff, and that the latter contained much that displeased him. Hamann attacked reason in the name of divine revelation; Vico's theory of history depended on a vitalistic concept of social authority, developed in time by divine providence; and Herder's notion of national *Volksgeist* had disturbing cosmological and political implications. Yet when we read these thinkers ourselves, without Berlin's assistance, what strikes us first is how different the kernels appear, and how firmly bound they are to the chaff. I am not raising the pedantic objection that Isaiah Berlin might have misinterpreted this or that aspect of the Counter-Enlightenment. I am asserting that the fundamental core of the Counter-Enlightenment actually was its hostility to enlightenment—as such. And therefore it was hostile to the basic moral and political values which Berlin himself defended.

There is, to begin, the problem of religion. Whatever their personal beliefs about the divine, Vico, Herder, and Hamann all equated religious life with social life. That is, they believed that society lives primarily through its religion, and cannot be conceived apart from it. This is not a liberal conception of church and state, to say the least. Another problem is that of social pluralism. While Vico and Herder certainly saw the human species as a patchwork of different nations and culture, they were also openly hostile to the idea of diversity *within* those cultures. What Vico and Herder found so contemptible in Imperial Rome and modern society was precisely their cosmopolitanism, which they blamed for moral collapse and spiritual anomie. And, finally, there is the problem of reason itself. I think it is fair to say that Vico, Herder, and Hamann not only distrusted reason's tendency to trespass its proper boundaries; they saw it as a destructive force threatening the subrational or irrational ties that actually bind societies together. Those therefore must be protected from rational scrutiny, lest society enter what Vico called, in an evocative phrase, the "barbarism of reflection."

The one figure in the Counter-Enlightenment for whom Berlin felt deep disgust was Joseph de Maistre, the eighteenth-century Catholic reactionary whom Berlin placed at the origins of fascist thought. But Maistre's central doctrines are not very easy to distinguish from the pluralism of Berlin's foxes; Maistre simply pushed them to a frightening extreme. Maistre, like Vico, thought that philosophy was a threat to the well-ordered society, calling it "an essentially disorganizing power." And, in a famous statement to which Herder might have assented, Maistre wrote that "in the course of my life I have seen Frenchmen, Italians, Russians, etc.; I know, too, thanks to Montesquieu, that one can be a Persian. But as for man, I declare that I have never met him in my life; if he exists, he is unknown to me."[3] To which must be added the following sentence: "Just as nature does not produce flowers and fruits of a general character, nor general plants and animals, but produces particular plant and animal types, so does the creative power in history produce only folk types."[4] That sentence is not from Maistre, or even from Herder; it is from *Rome and Jerusalem* by Moses Hess.

I am being provocative, of course. It would be absurd to ignore the profound gulf separating Maistre

3. Quoted in *The Crooked Timber of Humanity*, p. 100.

4. Moses Hess, *Rome and Jerusalem* (Bloch, 1918), p. 121.

from Vico, Herder, Hamann, and Hess. But whatever does separate them, it is not the principle of pluralism, nor a theory of reason, nor the character of hedgehogs and foxes. Vico, Herder, Hamann, and Hess are lambs; Joseph de Maistre is a wolf. That is the essential difference.

The distinction between wolves and lambs goes to the very heart of the liberal tradition. *Homo homini lupus*: because man can be a wolf to man, Enlightenment liberals worked for a political order that would protect basic human decencies, and they demolished justifications of arbitrary cruelties that rested on appeals to revelation and tradition. Isaiah Berlin himself joined this effort in the 1950s, when he took on those modern justifications of cruelty based on historical necessity or utopian visions of positive liberty. But Berlin, like many liberals today, was also haunted by the worry that liberalism's attachment to universal principles, discovered through reason, somehow rendered it less liberal and tolerant than it ought to be. Although he rejected the Marxist contention that history trumps all claims of reason, he was more than willing to entertain the appeal of cultural pluralists who wished to exempt the practices of certain nations and religions from rational scrutiny. So strong was his sympathy for cultural pluralists, genuine or fraudulent, that it drove him into the questionable company of the Counter-Enlightenment in search of intellectual support.

The liberal character, like all characters, has its characteristic weaknesses. Liberals are susceptible to paralyzing self-doubt and overestimate the goodness of

man. Too often, they are willing lambs. But more than
that, liberals are also prone to turn one of their own
cardinal virtues—open-mindedness—into a vice by
misapplying it. This tendency was once described with
malicious gusto by George Eliot in one of her essays.
There she described a modern man, who, she writes,
"may be known in conversation by the cordiality with
which he assents to indistinct, blurred statements: say
that black is black, he will shake his head and hardly
think it; say that black is not so very black, he will
reply, 'Exactly.' He has no hesitation, if you wish it,
even to get up at a public meeting and express his conviction that at times, and within certain limits, the radii
of a circle have a tendency to be equal; but, on the
other hand, he would urge that the spirit of geometry
may be carried a little too far."[5] This is a comic portrait, but there is truth in it. In his desire to be openminded and pluralistic, Isaiah Berlin convinced himself
that the Enlightenment had pushed the principle of
reason too far, and that there might be something to
the Counter-Enlightenment claim that, seen in cultural
perspective, black deeds are not really as black as they
appear.

In my view, he was mistaken on both counts. That liberalism, like any political doctrine, needs to be applied
with moderation and prudence was self-evident to
all the great liberal thinkers. But it is an error to think
that the Counter-Enlightenment's attack on reason,

---

5. George Eliot, *Essays* (London: Penguin, 1990), pp. 389–390.

individualism, and modernity were merely inspired by fox-like cunning or by skeptical appreciation of humanity's crooked timber. And it is an even greater error to think that their ideas are compatible with liberalism and can make it more decent. Though they spoke with the tongues of foxes, their words only provide comfort to the wolves, who gain strength in the twilight. A wise liberal will study such thinkers, and learns by studying their passions and obsessions. But friendship? That is impossible.

STEVEN LUKES

An Unfashionable Fox

WHILE WORKING ON a book on "individualism"[1] I recall telling Isaiah Berlin that I had found eleven distinct
senses of that protean concept. He outfoxed me, com-
menting, "That's rather mean!" In rather the same
spirit I want to begin by making the same observation
about his famous distinction (drawn from the Greek
poet Archilochus) between the hedgehog and the fox.
I reject the hedgehog-like view that there is only one
distinction here—only one kind of hedgehog and one
kind of fox. For among humans there are many kinds
of hedgehogs and many kinds of foxes. On some of
these Berlin fixed his attention, exposing the moral
and political costs of adopting the hedgehogs' limited
vision, while exploring the world-views of thinkers he
recognized as fellow foxes. But there are other kinds
of (presently fashionable) foxes he did not recognize
as his fellows, with whom he had no elective affinity.
I shall conclude by saying something about them and
address the question, "What kind of a fox was he?"

---

1. Steven Lukes, *Individualism* (Oxford: Blackwell, 1973).

43

Allow me to offer you a preliminary typology of hedgehogs—thinkers who, in Berlin's words, "relate everything to a single central vision, one system more or less coherent or articulate, in terms of which they understand, think and feel—a single, universal, organizing principle in terms of which alone all that they are and say has significance."[2] I suggest there are at least four varieties, four species of this genus (because of time constraints we must be mean).

First there are what we may call the *positivist* hedgehogs. They believe that "history could (and should) be made scientific," on the model of natural science (or what natural science is taken to be). Thus Auguste Comte, writes Berlin, "tried to turn history into sociology," but perhaps of all thinkers Marx took this program most seriously, making "the bravest, if one of the least successful, attempts to discover general laws which govern historical evolution." (This according to Berlin; I hereby forego the temptation to dispute this interpretation of Marx as positivist). Berlin remarks that Tolstoy:

> ... saw clearly that if history was a science, it must be possible to discover and formulate a set of true laws of history which, in conjunction with the data of empirical observation, would make prediction of the future (and "retrodiction" of the past) as feasible as it had become, say, in geology

---

2. Isaiah Berlin, *The Hedgehog and the Fox* (Mentor Books, New American Library, 1957), p. 7.

or astronomy. But he saw...that this had, in
fact, not been achieved...and reinforced his
thesis with arguments designed to show that the
prospect of achieving this goal was nonexistent;
and clinched the matter by observing that the ful-
fillment of this scientific hope would end human
life as we knew it."[3]

45

Tolstoy, by nature (on Berlin's account) a fox but
who believed in being a hedgehog, had insight into
what he saw as "permanently out of the reach of
science—the social, moral, political, spiritual worlds,
which cannot be sorted out and described and predicted by any science, because the proportion in them
of 'submerged,' uninspectable life is too high." Insight
into the nature and structure of these worlds required
a form of understanding which "distinguishes the real
from the sham, the worthwhile from the worthless,
that which can be done or borne from what cannot
be; and does so without giving rational grounds for its
pronouncements."[4]

But Berlin hunted other foxes of the anti-positivist
kind. Chief among these was, of course, Vico, the "true
father both of the modern concept of culture and of
what one might call cultural pluralism, according to
which each authentic culture has its own unique vision,
its own scale of values, which, in the course of development, is superseded by other visions and values, but

---

3. Berlin, *The Hedgehog and the Fox*, pp. 25–26.

4. Berlin, *The Hedgehog and the Fox*, pp. 106–107.

never wholly so" and of historical anthropology and the "forgotten anticipator of the German historical school" whose distinctive method was imaginative insight to decipher the meaning of conduct and language different from our own, the faculty of *fantasia* which we employ to "hear men's voices, to conjecture (on the basis of such evidence as we can gather) what may have been their experience, their forms of expression, their values, outlook, aims, ways of living."[5] Berlin's claim for Vico was that he "uncovered a species of knowing not previously clearly discriminated, the embryo that later grew into the ambitious and luxuriant plant of German historicist *Verstehen*—empathetic insight, intuitive sympathy, historical *Einfühlung*, and the like"—a sense of knowing that "is basic to all humane studies: the sense in which I know what it is to be poor, to fight for a cause, to belong to a nation, to join or abandon a church or a party, to feel nostalgia, terror, the omnipresence of a god, to understand a gesture, a work of art, a joke, a man's character, that one is transformed or lying to oneself."[6] This, Berlin argued, was a discovery of the first order, providing an escape route from the hegemonic hedgehogs of positivism.

Second, there are what we might label *universalist* hedgehogs, or, better perhaps (using Lovejoy's term),

5. Isaiah Berlin, "Giambattista Vico and Cultural History," in *The Crooked Timber of Humanity: Chapters in the History of Ideas*, edited by Henry Hardy (Knopf, 1991), pp. 59–60, 62–63, 64–65.

6. Isaiah Berlin, "Vico's Concept of Knowledge," in *Against the Current: Essays in the History of Ideas*, edited by Henry Hardy (London: The Hogarth Press, 1979), p. 116.

uniformitarian hedgehogs. They hold with Hume that "mankind is much the same in all times and places," with Locke that, "Vertues and Vices . . . for the most part are much the same everywhere" and with Voltaire that "morality is the same in all civilized nations." They may like Voltaire catalog the widely varying customs found in past and present societies, but only with the purpose of illustrating the unvarying contrast between the civilized and the barbarians, between what is more and what is less enlightened. Berlin comments that Voltaire's conception of enlightenment as identical in essentials wherever it is attained seems to lead to the inescapable conclusion that, in his view, Byron would have been happy at table with Confucius, and Sophocles would have felt completely at ease in quattrocento Florence, and Seneca in the *salon* of Madame du Deffand or at the court of Frederick the Great.

To the universalist hedgehog cultural differences merely conceal transculturally invariant interests and motives, and ways of behaving; and they have no bearing on our moral or aesthetic or political judgments which, although they must arise in a particular cultural context, can be framed in abstract, context-free terms, according to which different ways of life, and their practices, can, in turn, be ranked.

For Berlin the fox who exploded this set of ideas was Herder. For Herder:

> There is a plurality of incommensurable cultures. To belong to a given community, to be connected with its members by indissoluble and impalpable

ties of common language, historical memory, habit, tradition and feeling, is a basic human need, no less natural than that for food or drink or security or procreation.[7]

So cultural differences run deep, shaping thought, perception and belief, and there are no culture-independent criteria of progress (as was believed in eighteenth-century Paris, and even Herder himself half accepted); every human achievement and every human society is to be judged by its own internal standards. For Herder cosmopolitanism meant shedding what made individuals most human; and every image of *Humanität* was culturally *sui generis*.

This fox-like vision Berlin traced forward to cultural nationalism in the Austro-Hungarian, Turkish and Russian empires and thence to political nationalism in Austria and Germany and, by infectious reaction, elsewhere; and it is clearly at the root of what we today call identity politics. Here, I believe, Berlin took over, too uncritically, Herder's unremittingly holistic view of cultures. (This sort of poor man's sociology is all too common among present-day writers impressed by cultural differences). He never asked to what extent cultures are always clusters or assemblages of heterogeneous elements of varying origins, which differ from one another more as ecosystems or climactic regions than as nation states divided by

---

7. Berlin, "The Counter-Enlightenment," in *Against the Current*, p. 12.

frontiers. He had, at least in this sector of his thinking, a mosaic or patchwork rather than a hodge-podge view of cultures.[8]

49

Third, there are what I shall call *rationalist* hedgehogs. They are, once more, to be found among the *philosophes*, the majority of whom, he claims, believed that "the true, the only true, ends that all wise men sought at all times—in art, in thought, in morals and manners" were "timeless and universal, known to all reasonable men" and that "the light of the truth, *lumen naturalis*, is everywhere and always the same, even if men were often too wicked or stupid or weak to discover it, or if they did, to lead their lives by its radiance."[9] Some, like Voltaire and Rousseau, were of course pessimistic about progress towards truth, virtue and happiness. Others, like Condorcet (for whom these were linked in an "indissoluble chain") and Helvétius were more sanguine. He qualifies this caricatural description by mentioning various forms of skepticism abroad in the eighteenth century, among the *philosophes* themselves as well as beyond. But what he called "the central tradition of the Enlightenment" invested massively, he plausibly claimed, in such hopes.

And here we come to Berlin's favorite foxes: Hamann, passionate Christian pietist, violently opposed to all

---

8. For an elaboration of this distinction (which implicitly refers to Salman Rushdie's version of the "hodge-podge" view), see the introduction to Christian Joppke and Steven Lukes, editors, *Multicultural Questions* (Oxford University Press, 1999).

9. Berlin, "Giambattista Vico and Cultural History," p. 52.

abstract and conceptual thought and apostle of feeling and direct perception through faith; and Joseph de Maistre, whose world was "much more realistic and more ferocious than that of the Romantics." For Maistre reason was but a "flickering light." He exhibited "the doctrine of violence at the heart of things, the belief in the power of dark forces, the glorification of chains as alone capable of curbing man's self-destructive instincts, and using them for his salvation, the appeal to blind faith against reason, the belief that only what is mysterious can survive ... the doctrine of blood and self-immolation ... of the absurdity of liberal individualism, and above all of the subversive influence of uncontrolled critical intellectuals." All this, Berlin observed, was at the heart of modern totalitarianism and sounded the earliest note of modern militant anti-rational Fascism.[10]

Then, alongside and in succession to Hamann were other anti-rationalist German Romantic thinkers; and then, of course, Sorel, for whom violence was the prelude to regeneration and for whom irrational susceptibility to myths was inseparable from collective action but who was "a penetrating and cruel critic of the vices of parliamentary democracy and bourgeois humanitarianism."[11] These too were his fellow foxes, in whom he was interested, as he explained in an interview with me, because they are "... hostile thinkers. I am against them,

---

10. Berlin, "Joseph de Maistre and the Origins of Fascism," in *The Crooked Timber of Humanity*, pp. 158, 127.

11. Berlin, "Georges Sorel," in *Against the Current*, p. 327.

but they said things that make one think."[12] As Michael Ignatieff remarks, "Berlin was the only liberal thinker of real consequence to take the trouble to enter the mental worlds of liberalism's sworn enemies."[13]

Fourth, there are what we will call the *monist* hedgehogs—and here we come to what was perhaps the center of Berlin's preoccupations (if a fox, and he clearly was a fox—but I will come to that—can be allowed to have a central preoccupation): what he variously calls "monism," the *"philosophia perennis"* and "the old perennial belief in the possibility of realizing ultimate harmony."[14] What, according to Berlin, does a monist believe? That "all the positive values in which men have believed must, in the end, be compatible, and perhaps even entail one another." And, to illustrate the Enlightenment's alleged commitment to this belief, he cites Condorcet—"one of the best men who ever lived"— who famously wrote that "Nature binds truth, happiness and virtue together by an indissoluble chain."[15] (He came to see that he had been unfair to Condorcet's nuanced views on these matters). Other *philosophes*, he suggests, thought similarly of liberty, equality and justice. Implicit in this belief, he thought, is a much more dangerous one, that "it is in principle possible to

---

12. "Isaiah Berlin in Conversation with Steven Lukes," *Salmagundi*, No. 120 (Fall 1998), p. 90.

13. Michael Ignatieff, *Isaiah Berlin: A Life* (Henry Holt, 1998), p. 249.

14. Berlin, "The Pursuit of the Ideal," in *The Crooked Timber*, p. 17.

15. Isaiah Berlin, "Two Concepts of Liberty," in *Four Essays on Liberty* (Oxford University Press, 1969), p. 167.

discover a harmonious pattern in which all values are reconciled, and that it is towards this unique goal that we must make; that we can uncover some single central principle that shapes this vision, a principle which, once found, will govern our lives."[16] And this latter belief, he famously asserted, is responsible more than any other for "the slaughter of individuals on the altars of the great historical ideals,"[17] including liberty itself. (More than any other? Here is quite a different account of the ideological roots of modern totalitarianism, in striking contrast with what he says about de Maistre, the Romantics and Sorel).

Against this bundle of beliefs he defended what he called the pluralism of values—the position that we are "faced with choices between ends equally ultimate, and claims equally absolute, the realization of some of which must inevitably involve the sacrifice of others"; that "the ends of men are many, and not all of them are in principle compatible with each other," so that "the possibility of conflict—and of tragedy—can never be wholly eliminated from human life, either personal or social" and "the necessity of choosing between absolute claims is then an inescapable characteristic of the human condition" and that "human goals are many, not all of them commensurable, and in perpetual rivalry with one another." For in the end "men choose between ultimate values; they choose as they do because their life and thought are determined by fundamental categories and

---

16. Introduction to Berlin, *Four Essays on Liberty*, p. lv.

17. Berlin, "Two Concepts of Liberty," p. 167.

concepts that are, at any rate over long stretches of time and space, a part of their being and thought and sense of their own identity, part of what makes them human."[18]

Several of his favorite foxes exhibited value pluralism: Machiavelli, who saw that for the Prince two moral outlooks and sets of virtues, the Christian and the pagan, "were not merely in practice but in principle incompatible," thereby planting "a permanent question mark in the path of posterity," stemming from his recognition that "ends equally ultimate, equally sacred, may contradict each other, that entire systems of value may come into collision without possibility of rational arbitration... as part of the normal human situation."[19] And John Stuart Mill, the "disciple who quietly left the fold," "acutely aware of the many-sidedness of the truth and of the irreducible complexity of life," whose "conception of man was... deeper, and his vision of history and life wider and less simple than that of his utilitarian predecessors and liberal followers."[20]

There is much more to say about this distinction between monism and pluralism but I would here just like to observe (in a fox-like spirit) that there are various different ideas here and they do not obviously all hang together. So a monist can deny and a pluralist assert at least the following different things: that values are plural

---

18. Berlin, "Two Concepts of Liberty," pp. 168–169, 171–172.

19. Berlin, "The Originality of Machiavelli," in *Against the Current*, pp. 69, 74–75.

20. Isaiah Berlin, "John Stuart Mill and the Ends of Life" (London: The Council of Christians and Jews, 1959), pp. 6, 21, 34.

—that is, diverse, not forms or derivatives of, or reducible to, a single value or set of values; that they can be incompatible, that is, not jointly realizable within the confines of a single life or single society; that they can contradict one another (as military glory contradicts Christian meekness, or deference to hierarchy comradely equality); that they can be incomparable—there may be no relevant respect in relation to which one valued alternative can be judged in relation to another; and they can be incommensurable, in the separate senses that there is no common standard in terms of which to rank them, or that to rank them is to misunderstand or corrupt them.

So Berlin was a critic of positivism and scientism, and yet he remained staunchly loyal to his early empiricist outlook and was never much troubled by post-empiricist philosophies of science or the hermeneutic circle—by the thought that all the facts are theory-laden or that interpretations are mutually interlocking or that they might be indeterminate. His views about these matters were, in practice, rather Popperian. He remained, as Stuart Hampshire well put it, "a convinced and calm empiricist, who insisted that the stuff of our day-to-day experience, whether in personal experience or in politics, is the true stuff of reality. . . . He took the furniture of the world, both the natural and the social furniture, medium-sized objects on a human scale, to be entirely real and to exist more or less as we perceive them."[21] So, although he had a

---

21. Stuart Hampshire, address delivered at the Commemoration in the Sheldonian Theatre, Oxford, March 21, 1998.

prejudice against the subject of sociology, he was never inclined to follow foxes like Paul Feyerabend or Clifford Geertz into radical anarchist or "anti-anti-relativist" doubts about objectivity in the social sciences, let alone science in general.

He was against uniformitarian universalism. Yet despite his extremely sympathetic account of Herder, he was himself never attracted to anything like social constructionism—to, for instance, the view of Richard Rorty that "we must avoid the embarrassment of the universalist claim that 'human being'... names an unchanging essence, an ahistorical natural kind with a permanent set of intrinsic features," that "socialization, and thus historical circumstance, goes all the way down—that there is nothing 'beneath' socialization or prior to history which is definatory of the human"— that "the self, the human subject is simply whatever acculturation makes of it."[22] Berlin believed that human nature set limits to the intelligible ends that human beings can pursue, so, in his interview with me, he remarks that "the number of ends that human beings can pursue is not infinite... in practice human beings would not be human if that were so."[23]

---

22. Richard Rorty, *Essays on Heidegger and Others* (Cambridge University Press, 1991), p. 77; "Feminism and Pragmatism," *Radical Philosophy*, No. 59 (Autumn 1991), p. 5; *Contingency, Irony and Solidarity* (Cambridge University Press, 1989), pp. xiii, 64.

23. "Isaiah Berlin in Conversation with Steven Lukes," pp. 103–104. On this issue, Michael Ignatieff comments (in *Isaiah Berlin: A Life*, pp. 249–250):

"...we are moral beings: we would not qualify as human if moral considerations, however false or inadequate, were absent from our deliberations. And from this common ground—of a shared body and

56 He was a critic of Enlightenment rationalism (as he construed it)—and also of what he saw as the excessive rationalism of some contemporary liberal thinkers, notably John Rawls,[24] yet he firmly believed in the place of reason in ethics and in the objectivity of values, and he was never attracted by the various varieties of subjectivism and emotivism in ethics or in later years by existentialism. And he certainly showed no sympathy for those contemporary post-Nietzschean, post-modernist foxes who have taken the notion of incommensurability far further than he ever did, as when Lyotard says that "to speak is to fight" and suggests that there is an irreducible incommensurability across discourses and narratives since these "define what has the right to be said and done in the culture in question, and since they are themselves a part of that culture, they are legitimated thereby."[25]

And he was a value pluralist, yet he came to attach much importance to distinguishing his view from relativism. Pluralism, he insisted, is not relativism—which we could (following the happy phrase of the late

---

a shared language of moral discourse—we know the inhuman when we encounter it. He had no convincing argument as to why men and women, who had imbibed the culture of Western universalism through Goethe and Schiller, should have treated their fellows as so much vermin. All he could say was that to regard human beings as vermin was to reason from demonstrably false premises. But why such reasoning should have become persuasive to the entire political class of a great nation, and to millions of their supporters in Europe, he could not say. But then, who can?"

24. See "In Conversation with Steven Lukes," p. 113.

25. Jean-François Lyotard, *La Condition Postmoderne* (Paris: Les éditions de minuit, 1979), pp. 23, 42–43.

Martin Hollis) encapsulate in the slogan "liberalism for the liberals, cannibalism for the cannibals."[26] His final position was, I believe, something like this: over large areas of our practical life, above all in the sphere of public policy, we engage in trade-offs, weighing goods and engaging in compromises that prevent intolerable alternatives from arising. But moral dilemmas and tragic choices are ineliminable. As Ignatieff well says, "Berlin made human dividedness, both inner and outer, the very rationale for a liberal polity. A free society was a good society because it accepted the conflict among human goods and maintained, through its democratic institutions, the forum in which this conflict could be managed peacefully."[27]

But I disagree with Ignatieff's view that Berlin, whose own self was "labile, multi-faceted" and "sharply divided," was "a fox who longed to be a hedgehog."[28] I would rather say that he remained what these days looks like a rather old-fashioned fox, who saw many things we hedgehogs wouldn't normally see: an empiricist, realist, objectivist, anti-irrationalist, anti-relativist fox.

---

26. Berlin's repeated attempts to define a pluralism untainted by relativism date from his reaction to a review of his *Vico and Herder* by Arnaldo Momigliano in *The New York Review*, November 11, 1976. For a discussion and brief assessment of these attempts see Steven Lukes, "Berlin's Dilemma," *Times Literary Supplement*, March 27, 1998, pp. 8–9.

27. Ignatieff, *Isaiah Berlin: A Life*, p. 203.

28. Ignatieff, *Isaiah Berlin: A Life*, p. 203.

Hedgehogs and Foxes

AILEEN KELLY: In Mark Lilla's criticism I heard a sense of cultural desperation, an impression that, at the end of the twentieth century and in postmodern culture, we're on the edge. We're about to sink into the abyss. Hilaire Belloc's old maxim, "Always keep a-hold of Nurse, for fear of finding something worse," seems to be a fair description of the implied response. In other words, that we may have advanced a little beyond the Enlightenment, but it's still the safest framework we have for our thinking, and that there are many far worse.

I feel that this is both monistic and unrealistic. We can't go back to a scheme with the cracks in it that Berlin has revealed. What he actually said was that we are heirs to two traditions, and that we therefore shift uneasily from foot to foot. We are heirs to the Counter-Enlightenment, to Romanticism, and to everything else that has happened since the Enlightenment. We cannot now credibly return to one single tradition. We cannot be consistent monists, even if our best friends may wish to be. And I believe it should be remembered that he knew that this position of moving from one foot to another was extremely unsatisfactory, but nevertheless thought it to be the only thing we could reasonably do.

MARK LILLA: I think you're probably right that this was Isaiah Berlin's view—that we can't go back—though I should point out that it reflects a kind of historical necessity to which he was generally hostile. Moreover, that was the attitude of the Counter-Enlightenment toward the Enlightenment, which, in my view, Berlin accepted uncritically. The Counter-Enlightenment portrayed the Enlightenment as coming at the end of a certain history, and whether it was a good thing or a bad thing, or a partially good thing, something new had to come after it. And it's that notion of something inevitably coming after the Enlightenment that I think he accepted.

No, I certainly don't feel the sense of crisis. On the contrary, what I find suspicious in so many Counter-Enlightenment thinkers is *their* ever-present sense of crisis, their belief that we are somehow living at the edge of an abyss because modernity, technology, liberalism, and modern anomie have driven us there. This leads to a misplaced open-mindedness toward certain ideas which promise withdrawal from the abyss but actually lead in a direction quite different from where Berlin himself wanted to go.

STEVEN LUKES: I agree very much with Mark's statement that Isaiah Berlin read the Enlightenment through the Counter-Enlightenment. As he said to me, he found thinkers who were too sympathetic rather boring. So he didn't read Enlightenment thinkers with attention and certainly didn't write about them very much. He was much more interested in how they were perceived.

But I disagree with Mark in that I don't think he ever supposed that this totalitarian danger was actually present in their thought. He thought it was something implicit in their monism, of which they were themselves unaware. But it was there to be discovered and elicited later.

That's what makes his interpretation so paradoxical. Above all, identifying the roots of totalitarianism in a thinker like Condorcet is a very striking, bold assertion. But what I find to be a big hole in the argument is he never really explains why. If you hold to either monism or pluralism, why should the terrible or desirable political consequences follow? This is a step he never takes. He never says why, for example, if I believe that values are somehow irreconcilable in a single scheme, this will protect me from totalitarian inclinations. Nor does he explain why the belief in harmonizing values should be so dangerous. He can of course point to the example to which he always did point, namely Marxism. But there's no explanation really of why this thought structure should have these political consequences.

MR. LILLA: Another difference between Berlin and the enlightened figures he admired is that they placed the source of evil in different things. There's a strong sense in the Enlightenment of the problem of evil, though it is divided over the degree to which all human beings are

62

evil. Some Enlightenment thinkers thought that getting rid of the Church and superstition would turn men into lambs. But in someone like Voltaire there's also a very strong sense of the fall and original sin, though without God, if you like. That is why among liberals inspired by the Enlightenment there is a strong sense of what needs to be done culturally and socially in order to protect people from each other. But if one starts searching for the causes of evil in ideas, rather than in human nature, one is tempted to think that if we just change our ideas—about our attachments to family, nation, religion—we can go a long way to rooting out evil. I think Isaiah Berlin may have succumbed to this temptation.

RONALD DWORKIN: Aileen, you say that we can't go back because Isaiah Berlin pointed to what you described as cracks in the Enlightenment. Could you say a bit more about that? What were these cracks?

MS. KELLY: I think we tend to lose sight of the fact that Berlin also believed that extreme pluralism, extreme particularism, could lead to equally disastrous consequences. Perhaps regrettably, he didn't spell out how this might happen, but with reference to his own thought he was very careful to stress what he saw as fundamental differences between his pluralism and a relativist stance. The argument that he was "against" the Enlightenment doesn't take any account of the central importance he attached to objective knowledge as a self-sufficient value. His belief in the emancipating role of knowledge, the emancipating role of science, is completely in the spirit of the Enlightenment: it is in fact the core of the Enlightenment vision. The cracks he saw in that vision derived from its over-optimistic faith that progress in rational understanding would lead to the resolution of all human problems. He believed that this rationalist universalism is not grounded in our moral experience, which leads us instead to a sense of the incommensurabilities between some ultimate values. It is on this issue that Berlin parted company with mainstream Enlightenment thought, which cannot be reconciled with what has been called his ethical realism—his view that moral judgments must start from the particularities of concrete situations rather than from universal precepts.

The problem with the Enlightenment's heritage is that the cracks are increasingly evident: we have come more and more to recognize that moral and historical experience do not support its optimism about the power of reason. This recognition began with insights of the Counter-Enlightenment and Romanticism which, however repellent some of their representatives may have been, were still genuine insights. Again, I emphasize the importance of Berlin's remark at the end of his essay, "The Pursuit of the Ideal," that whether we like it or not, we are now heirs to two traditions. I tried to bring out the significance of his essays on Russian thinkers as illustrations of this view: some of the Russian pluralists with whom he has most affinity drew for example on Romantic and Hegelian thought, but equally on Enlightenment ideas. Berlin sees the fact that we have inherited all these complex and sometimes mutually contradictory perceptions and perspectives as rather frightening but also rather exhilarating. While he believed, I think, that the main strand of liberalism still holds desperately onto the certainties of Enlightenment universalism—basically as a case of "keeping a-hold of Nurse"—he regarded it as clear that we can no longer credibly construct our outlook on those certainties.

MICHAEL WALZER: I want to question the idea that Isaiah Berlin read the Enlightenment only through the Counter-Enlightenment. He did that sometimes, when he was reading Counter-Enlightenment figures. But he also made what is after all a standard liberal criticism of the Enlightenment, which focuses on the very close connection between Enlightenment and despotism. Marx's dictatorship of the proletarian is a latter-day version of enlightened despotism. It is the despotism of an enlightened, universal class, and Marx is very much an Enlightenment figure. And there is a liberal critique of all this that tries to explain it in terms of the arrogance of rationalism. It's not the skepticism or the tolerance of the Enlightenment that is blamed, but precisely the claim to know with certainty, to be definitively enlightened vis-à-vis the ignorant or fanatic others, as Marx thought he was, and then to be prepared to use coercive force, the powers of the state, to enact an enlightened politics. And that's not something that requires us to worry about the ancestors or the posterity of the Enlightenment; it is a feature of eighteenth-century enlightened philosophy that the *philosophes* made alliances with despotism.

MR. LILLA: Michael has a point. I think that's a feature of the Enlightenment, but a minor one in my view. Coming back to something Aileen Kelly just said, I want to emphasize that I think Berlin accepted the Counter-Enlightenment's view that its problem was the Enlightenment. It's true that we learned something from Romanticism, and in a sense Romanticism is now part of us. But where Romanticism got things wrong was in thinking that its problem was with the Enlightenment. Its problem was with life. And we all have problems with life.

THOMAS NAGEL: I want to say something in response to the question that Steven Lukes raised about why Berlin thought there was a natural connection between monism and tyranny and the abuses that he associated with it. It might look—and I actually think that Michael Walzer's remark suggests this—as though it were a bad argument, based on the fact that the worst horrors of the twentieth century have been carried out in the name of monistic values. It simply doesn't follow from the connection in that direction, that the connection goes in the other direction, that every monistic value is going to lead to horrors.

I think that Berlin's reason for thinking that there was a strong association in that other direction, one which he may never have expressed but which was clearly implicit in his writings, is a kind of moral empiricism. He thought that as you could trust what you observed about middle-sized objects, you could trust basic moral instincts about the unacceptability of

66 cruelty and of the sacrifice of an innocent individual for a large good. The trouble with monistic ideologies or conceptions is that they tend to provide too much leverage for overriding those immediate moral instincts. If you have a pluralistic disposition, you'll be much more inclined to just trust them. I think that is an important insight.

MR. LUKES: I think that's right, but on the other hand, going back to the Enlightenment, it seems to me that that thought is an Enlightenment thought if any thought is. I mean, almost all Enlightenment moral philosophers with very few exceptions believed that sympathy and pity were natural to man. So if you're going to argue this you have to see its source in the Enlightenment, I think.

MR. DWORKIN: It's also the case, isn't it, that some natural instincts are not so good, and it might be good to have a lever for overriding them. That capacity for criticism of the natural was certainly an important part of the Enlightenment ideal.

CHARLES TAYLOR: I think Aileen Kelly is absolutely right. I would like to disagree a bit with Mark Lilla, because I think we need to get away from the idea that we're either basically with the Enlightenment or with the Counter-Enlightenment. I think Berlin's view is that neither of these perspectives alone will suffice. We need to learn from both.

Now, why is that so? Why doesn't the Enlightenment suffice, even with all the defenses of it already mentioned?

I think one of the things we learned from the Enlightenment is that we're always going to be creating a new future. We can't go back to the idea of there being a sacred order in which everything has to reproduce itself. And in that context, an insufficient understanding of the breadth of human motivation and human values can lead the people who are creating social plans or carrying them out to do some horrifying things. So we need an understanding of the tremendous palette of human motivation, and we find it in people like Herder, Hamann, and others. Monism, in order to fit everything together, has to forget nine-tenths of these motivations and values. We need anti-monism to avoid this over simplification. We may not like some Counter-Enlightenment thinkers, but we need their insights as well as Enlightenment ones.

RICHARD BERNSTEIN [Department of Philosophy, New School University]: I agree that this contrast of the Enlightenment and Counter-Enlightenment is something that would make Berlin very uneasy, and it does seem to me mistaken. I want to address Mark Lilla's argument on one point. You're basically accusing Berlin of cleaning up the Counter-Enlightenment and extracting what is positive, and I want to accuse you of cleaning up the Enlightenment on an issue that was very important to Berlin and that has not yet been mentioned—that is Jews and Jewishness.

Here it seems to me one either has to say that the

record of the Enlightenment is very complex, or it's absolutely terrible. Take a figure like Kant in *Religion within the Limits of Reason Alone*. Here is a great statement of reason, of morality and so forth, but if read carefully it's horrendous on the issue of Jews and Judaism. They are not part of the universal religion. Insofar as Christianity is to be redeemed, it is because it's a universal. And it seems to me that Berlin's sensitivity to dark sides, which I think Aileen Kelly was talking about, is relevant here. This is very important in defending his own kind of pluralism. We need a much more complex story than that happy one of reasonableness, sympathy, and toleration, because the prejudices, at least on the religious issue, are very, very strong.

MR. LILLA: I think Richard Bernstein has said something very important here. He's referring to a passage in *Religion within the Limits of Reason Alone* where Kant speaks of the "euthanasia of Judaism," which is a quite chilling passage. I in fact wish that Berlin had written more explicitly about the problem of Judaism than he did, because I happen to think that a lot of his writing is about that. Had he done so, I think he would have seen the Counter-Enlightenment with different eyes. I have often wondered, when reading Berlin on the Enlightenment, why doesn't he talk about Mendelssohn? Where is Lessing? What about Diderot and the *Supplement to Bougainville's Voyage*? Ideas of toleration of other nations and religions were obviously very dear to most of the Enlightenment. Many were only honored in the breach, because there were areas of social life where no one imagined these principles could be extended. But the grounds for later criticism derive directly from the Enlightenment.

Part II

PLURALISM

RONALD DWORKIN

Do Liberal Values Conflict?

YESTERDAY WE EXPLORED Isaiah Berlin's ideas about value pluralism through the lens of intellectual history. This morning we're going to be talking about his ideas as a distinct and important philosophical contribution, particularly to political philosophy.

I said yesterday that I thought that Berlin's ideas were growing in influence and would continue to do so. It's mainly in political philosophy, and in his idea of value pluralism, that I detect this growing and continuing influence. I'm going to read out a few sentences from his work, not connected sentences, but nevertheless adequate to suggest the considerable originality and interest of his thesis. He begins:

> What is clear is that values can clash. Values may easily clash within the breast of a single individual. And it does not follow that some must be true and others false. Both liberty and equality are among the primary goals pursued by human beings through many centuries. But total liberty for the wolves is death to the lambs. These collisions of

value are the essence of what they are and what we are.

If we are told that these contradictions will be solved in some perfect world in which all good things are harmonized in principle, then we must answer to those who say this that the meanings they attach to the names which for us denote the conflicting values are not ours. If they are transformed, it is into conceptions not known to us on earth. The notion of the perfect whole, the ultimate solution in which all good things coexist seems to me not merely unobtainable—that is a truism—but conceptually incoherent. Some among the great goods cannot live together. That is a conceptual truth. We are doomed to choose, and every choice may entail an irreparable loss.

Toward the end of his most famous essay, Berlin took this theme up again, but in a more minatory way. He recognized the appeal of the view that I just quoted him as declaring false, the appeal of the ideal of the perfect whole. He recognized its appeal as enduring and important. But he said that we must not yield to this impulse because (and I'm quoting again now), "to allow it to determine one's practice is a symptom of an equally deep and more dangerous moral and political immaturity."

Those are strong words, and they accuse me for what I am about to say. I shall try, nevertheless, to defend the holistic ideal that Berlin condemned in that grave way. But before I do, I should like to comment on his suggestion that this ideal is not only false but dangerous. There are indeed dangers in the hedgehog, but we must not forget that there are dangers in the fox as well. Just as tyrants have tried to justify great crimes by appealing to the idea that all moral and political values come together in some harmonious vision so transcendently important that murder is justified in its service, so other moral crimes have been justified by appeal to the opposite idea, that important political values necessarily conflict, that no choice among these can be defended as the only right choice, and that sacrifices in some of the things we care about are therefore inevitable.

Millions of people in this extraordinarily prosperous country are without decent lives or prospects. They have no health insurance, no adequate shelter, no jobs. How often have you heard it said, in answer to the charge that we must do something about this, that we cannot do too much because equality conflicts with liberty? That if we were to raise taxes to the level necessary to address poverty in any serious way, then we would be invading liberty? Or when we raise our eyes and look abroad, and see that in many parts of the world democracy is a joke, and we say there may not be much that we can do about this, but perhaps there is something, or when we look at the policies of the Taliban that deny medical care to women, and we recoil in horror, and we ask whether economic sanctions might do something about that, how often are we told that different cultures have different values, that it is a form of imperialism for us to insist that only our values are the right ones and that different values are mistaken? That we have our way of organizing a society, and the Taliban and other fundamentalist societies have theirs, and that at the end of the day all we can say is that a single society cannot incorporate all values, that they have made their choices among these, and that we have made ours?

The hedgehog need not be a tyrant—it's a great mistake, as Thomas Nagel pointed out yesterday, to think that because value monism may serve as the banner of tyranny it must always do so. Nor, of course, does value pluralism inevitably lead either to selfishness or indifference. But there are dangers on both sides, and whether the danger of the hedgehog is greater than the danger of the fox, as Berlin thought, seems very much to depend on time and place. In the mid-Fifties, when he wrote his famous lecture, Stalinism was rampant and the corpse of fascism still stank. It may very well have seemed, then, that civilization had more to fear from the hedgehog. But in contemporary America, and in other prosperous western democracies, that doesn't seem so plain: the fox may be the more threatening beast. Perhaps there's a pendulum that swings between these dangers.

Danger is not our main story, however. We want to consider how far Berlin was right, not about the good effects of his value pluralism, but about that doctrine's truth. I said that his is an original, powerful view, and I shall now try to explain why, not only because we must try to identify Berlin's claims accurately, but because the difficulties in his view only emerge once it is separated from more familiar claims. Berlin did not just insist, as so many writers now do, on the anthropological platitude that different societies are organized around very different values, and have difficulty in understanding one another. Nor does he simply combine that platitude, as so many others have, with the further skeptical claim that it makes no sense to speak of "objective" values at all. It is all too common, in the so-called postmodernist age, for scholars to claim that all values—liberal or fundamentalist or "Asian" values —are just subjective reactions or social creations, so that to think of these values as true or false is a deep philosophical mistake.

Berlin's view is more complex and interesting. He believed that values are indeed objective, but also that there are irresolvable conflicts among the true values. He argued, that is, not just that people are in conflict about what the truth is, but that there is conflict in the truth about these matters. That is why he spoke, as I quoted him, of conflict within a single breast, and we can capture his view most accurately by putting it in the first person. Suppose we ourselves set out to imagine a life that had everything in it that an ideal life should have. Or to construct a political constitution that would respect and enforce every important political value. We would be doomed, Berlin says, to fail in either of those projects.

The doom, he adds, is conceptual not contingent, and I must try to explain what he means by that further distinction, though I am not sure that I can show it to be as crisp as he thought. Obviously there are circumstances in which, for various accidental reasons, or because of injustice or wickedness, we cannot meet all our obligations to everyone. We might well not be able to rescue all the victims of a natural catastrophe before some die, for example. Churchill, in the exigencies of war, thought he had to sacrifice the citizens of Coventry, by not warning them of an impending air raid, in order to keep secret the fact that the Allies had broken a German secret code. If a nation has suffered from an unjust system of economic class, it might be necessary to limit liberty by abolishing private schools, at least for a generation, in order to help restore equality. These are cases in which, for different kinds of contingent or historical reasons, we cannot do all that we should.

Our values conflict, Berlin insists, in a deeper way than that, which is why he says that the ideal of harmony is not just unobtainable but "incoherent" because securing or protecting one value necessarily involves abandoning or compromising another. Our values conflict, that is, even if we get all the breaks. His examples help to clarify this distinction. You may feel that a life given over to spontaneity—following the urges and impulses of the moment—would be a glorious life to lead. But you may also feel the demands of the very different value of prudence: you may feel that a life committed to forethought, particularly for the needs and interests of others, would be a splendid life. But if you felt these twin appeals, you would have to cheat on one of them. You could not organize a life that made spontaneity dominant and yet left adequate room for prudence, or vice-versa. If you tried to bring these two values together in a single life the result would be a terrible mess: imagine the man who sets his wristwatch alarm to remind him when it is time for an hour of spontaneity. It won't work, and this is not just a matter of historical accident. The two values cannot be combined because they are, in the nature of the case, at war with each other.

We can easily find other examples that might have a greater purchase in your own life. Many people here, I expect, feel both the need for total absorption in some work or project and also a commitment to family responsibilities and pleasures that almost always pull in the opposite direction, and they know from experience how wrenching that conflict can sometimes be. Any choice someone in that position makes deprives his life, he thinks, of something essential to a good life, at least for him.

That last idea—that a conflict in important values involves some genuine and important damage—is central to Berlin's idea. He doesn't just mean that we cannot have everything that we want—that we cannot cram all the adventures and treats that we might want into a single life. That, as he says, is a truism. He means that we cannot bring into a single life everything that we think it makes a life defective not to have. What is the political analogue of that kind of failure? Of course a political community cannot achieve all the economic or cultural success that its citizens dream of, and of course its policies must sometimes disappoint some citizens through policies that benefit others. But political values name distinct responsibilities that a community has to its citizens, responsibilities that it is not simply disappointing but wrong to ignore or violate.

If we accept equality as a value, and we think that equality means that every citizen must have access to decent medical care, then we think that a prosperous community that allows some citizens to die for want of such care does them a grave wrong. If we accept liberty as a value, and we think that liberty is violated when rich people are taxed to provide more money for the poor, then we think that such taxes not only inconvenience the rich but wrong them. If we accept both equality and liberty, and think they have those implications, then we must think that a political community violates its responsibilities no matter what it does. It must choose, that is, not whether to wrong some group, but which group to wrong. That is the kind of conflict in political values that Berlin had in mind: the inevitability not of disappointment but of irredeemable moral stain.

His claim is a positive one—that values of different kinds do conflict in that tragic way—and we must take care to distinguish that positive view from the different and much less troubling observation that we are sometimes uncertain what our values demand of us. Thoughtful people are often uncertain about important political issues, and sometimes swing between opposite positions. We might begin thinking about the troubling issue of hate speech, for example, persuaded that any government that deprives anyone of free speech just because it disapproves of what he says, or because what he says is offensive to other people in the community, is acting illegitimately. And then we might listen a bit to what some people actually say—we might hear someone calling a black woman a nigger or telling some Jewish boy that Hitler was right and Jews should be gassed. And then we might have second thoughts: we might wonder whether free speech is really as important as we thought it was. Does a nation really compromise its legitimacy when it protects its most vulnerable citizens from that kind of attack? We might come first to one decision and then to the other: we might twist and turn and swing back and forth. Or we may collapse into indecision and find that, once we see the appeal of each side of the question, we simply cannot say, certainly with any confidence, what we think.

Berlin's claim has nothing to do with uncertainty, however, even that terminal kind of uncertainty. He claims, not that we often do not know what is the right decision, but that we often do know that no decision is right, which is a very different matter. So we must concentrate on the following question. When are we entitled, not simply to the negative idea that we do not know what it is right for us to do, but to the positive claim that we know that nothing that we do is right because, whatever we do, we do something wrong? The latter is an extremely ambitious claim: it purports to see to the bottom of a dilemma and see that there is no escape. Are we ever entitled to so ambitious a claim?

That depends on how we conceive the source of our responsibilities. Imagine yourself in the position of Abraham holding a knife over the breast of his son, Isaac. Suppose you believe that you have an absolute religious duty to obey your God, no matter what, and also an absolute moral duty not to injure your own child, no matter what, and you conceive these as duties independent in their source. Your theology insists both that God's authority in no way stems from the morality of his command and that morality's authority in no way stems from God's command. So long as you hold these convictions, you will be certain that you cannot avoid doing wrong. You are, as it were, subject to two sovereigns—God and morality—and in the tragic difficulty that, at least as you understand the situation, the command of each counts for nothing in the eyes of the other. You must choose, and each choice is a final and terrible disloyalty.

But is that really our situation in politics? I just said that we might be uncertain whether a government does wrong when it prohibits racist speech, or, on the contrary, it does wrong when it permits such speech. What further argument or reflection could replace this indecision with the positive conviction that government does wrong in either case? Our situation is very different from Abraham's: we are not beholden to two independent sovereign powers one of whom commands freedom of speech and the other of whom commands prosecution for racial insult. On the contrary, we are drawn to each of the rival positions through arguments that, if we were finally to accept them as authoritative, would release us from the appeal of the other one. If we really believe that citizens have a right to speak out even in ways that offend certain other citizens, then it would be odd also to believe that certain citizens have a right not to be offended by what other citizens say. And vice versa. We reach a political conviction in cases like this one, that is, not by discovering what some deity or authoritative body has commanded, which may easily produce a deep conflict, but by reflecting on and refining our own sense of the needs and values in play, and it is mysterious how that process could produce the kind of conflict Berlin claims. It seems puzzling how we could be persuaded, at one and the same time, that citizens have a right that racial insults not be uttered and that citizens have a right to utter racial insults. But unless we can finally accept both of these claims, and at the same time, we cannot claim the positive view that we violate citizens' rights whatever we do about racist speech.

Berlin would reply, I believe, that my account of how we might become uncertain about racist speech misses an important and pertinent fact—that we come to particular political controversies, like that one, encumbered by prior commitments to two abstract political values—liberty and equality—and that these values can and do act in the fashion of independent and competing sovereigns whose dictates may conflict. Indeed, as you know, he thought that the conflict between liberty and equality was a paradigm of value conflict, and that is also, as I suggested earlier, the alleged conflict that seems the most troublesome and dangerous in contemporary politics.

Do liberty and equality, now considered as abstract values, conflict in some way that explains why a political community might find itself not merely uncertain about what to do but certain that it must do wrong whatever it does? That depends on what we mean by liberty and by equality: it depends on how we conceive these abstract values. Berlin makes plain, in his famous essay about liberty, and in several other places as well, how he understands liberty. Liberty, he says, is freedom from the interference of others in doing whatever it is that you might wish to do. Now if that is how we understand liberty, then it's immediately apparent, isn't it, that liberty for the wolf is, as he says, death to the lamb. If that is what we mean by liberty, and we are committed to liberty so understood, then it is very plausible that this commitment will often conflict with other commitments, including even minimal egalitarian ones.

But are we committed to liberty understood in that way? Here is a rival conception of liberty, which I introduce into our conversation now just to show that our commitment to liberty is not automatically a commitment to liberty as Berlin understood it. We might say: liberty isn't the freedom to do whatever you might want to do; it's freedom to do whatever you like so long as you respect the moral rights, properly understood, of others. It's freedom to spend your own rightful resources or deal with your own rightful property in whatever way seems best to you. But so understood your liberty doesn't include freedom to take over the resources of someone else, or injure him in ways you have no right to do.

The lamb would be happier with that account of liberty, even though the wolf might not be. In any case, it is far from obvious that liberty understood in this different way would produce an inevitable conflict with equality. On the contrary, it seems unlikely that it would: if higher taxes are necessary to provide poorer citizens with what equality entitles them to have, then taxation for that purpose cannot count as an invasion of the liberty of the rich, because the property taken from them in taxes is not rightfully theirs. You might object—I expect that many of you will object—that I have begged the question against Berlin by defining liberty so that conflict is excluded from the start. But are you assuming that the only successful account of liberty is one that makes liberty independent of other values? One that allows us to decide what liberty requires, and when it has been sacrificed, without considering what rights—to equality or anything else—other people have? That begs the question in the opposite way— it assumes the picture of values as rival and independent sovereigns that makes conflict inevitable. In fact, we might say, the large question of value pluralism and conflict in politics that Berlin introduced just is the question of whether our political values are independent of one another in the way his definition of liberty insists, or whether they are interdependent in the way the rival conception of liberty I sketched suggests, and that is a question, as I shall now argue, not of dictionary definition or empirical discovery but of substantive moral and political philosophy.

Berlin warned us, in the passage I read out at the beginning, against such rival conceptions of liberty. If people come forward with ideas of liberty that don't produce conflicts, he said, we must tell them that the values they offer are not our values. But what does that mean? How do we decide that Berlin's definition of liberty, which produces conflict, is our notion of liberty and that rival accounts of liberty are foreign to us? He's not, of course, making a semantic point: he doesn't mean that the dictionary is decisive for his account. Indeed he recognizes that people use the words that name political concepts in many different ways. Nor can we conduct any analog to a laboratory experiment or investigation to see what liberty really is, the way we can conduct tests to decide what a lion is really made of. We can't conduct a DNA analysis of liberty. So how do we test Berlin's claim about what conception of liberty is ours, and which other conceptions are foreign? Can we look to history?

I suspect that some other members of the panel are already beginning to think that I am not giving history its due. I agree that the history of ideas is often crucial, and of course I agree that it was of the first importance for Berlin. But we must go beyond simply stating that history is crucial and try to see why and how it is crucial. I don't quite see how history can be decisive at this point in our argument. History may of course teach us that many societies whose reigning ideology denied any conflict among important values ended in some form of disaster, and that should no doubt put us on our guard. But history can't, it seems to me, help us further. We're trying to decide how better to understand the value of liberty—a value to which we take ourselves to be committed—in order to see whether we do wrong when, for example, we tax the well-off to redistribute to the poor. I see no substitute for treating that, at least in the main, as a moral rather than an historical issue.

How should we proceed? I said, you recall, that for Berlin a conflict in fundamental values, either personal or political, is not merely an inconvenience or disappointment but a kind of tragedy. When we face such a conflict, in his view, we inevitably suffer or commit some injury: we deprive our life of something we think it wounds a life not to have, or we wrong someone by denying him what it wrongs him not to have. We should begin there. We need an account of our political values that shows us why, in the case of each of our important values, that is so. Our leading political values—liberty, equality, democracy, justice and the rest—are general ideals we agree in endorsing in the abstract. That abstract agreement is important: we agree that it is essential that citizens not be coerced by government in offensive ways, that an economic structure treat people with equal concern, that the people govern themselves, and so forth. When we try to make these very abstract values more concrete, by deciding what forms of coercion are offensive, what distribution of resources does treat people with equal concern, what form of self government is possible, and so forth, we must respect and preserve that first understanding. We must formulate more precise conceptions of our values so as to show, more precisely, what the value we identified in the abstract really is. We need an account that shows us what is good about liberty or equality or democracy, so that we can see why any compromise of these values is not merely inconvenient but bad. Of course we will disagree at this point: we will each defend somewhat different, and perhaps very different, conceptions of liberty, equality, and the rest. But it is crucial that we each defend conceptions that, for us, carry the abstract value forward into the controversial conception, so as to make plain why what we regard as a compromise of fundamental values is, just in itself, something grave or at least bad.

We can therefore test a proposed conception of liberty—or of any other value—in the following way. We should ask whether the various actions that the proposed conception defines as violations of liberty are really bad or wrong—are really breaches of some special responsibility for which a state should feel remorse even when those breaches are necessary in order not to violate some supposed competing value. If not—if a state does not wrong any citizen when, according to the proposed definition, it invades his liberty—then the proposed conception of liberty is inadequate. It declares a violation when a violation is no wrong, and it therefore does not show us what the special importance of liberty is.

Does Berlin's account of liberty pass that test? Suppose I want to murder my critics. The law will stop me from doing that, and the law will therefore, on Berlin's account, compromise my liberty. Of course, everyone agrees that I must be stopped: those who defend Berlin's definition say that although my liberty has been invaded, the invasion is justified in this case, because the wrong done to me is necessary to prevent a greater wrong to others. In this case, they say, liberty is in conflict with other values and those other values must prevail. But I am asking whether the account of liberty that produces that alleged conflict is a successful account: if nothing wrong has taken place when I am prevented from killing my critics, then we have no reason for adopting a conception of liberty that describes the event as one in which liberty has been sacrificed. We are not, to repeat, required to describe it that way in virtue of what the word "liberty" means, or in virtue of any scientific discovery about the composition of liberty. A conception of liberty is an interpretive theory that aims to show us why it is bad when liberty is denied, and a conception of liberty is therefore unsuccessful when it forces us to describe some event as an invasion of liberty when nothing bad has happened.

So I ask you again: is there anything even *pro tanto* wrong in forbidding me to kill my critics? Of course, it would be better if no one wanted to injure any one else or any one else's property: it would be better if the criminal law was unnecessary. That is not the question, however. Given that some people do want to kill on some occasions, is any wrong done to them by preventing them from doing so? Do we have any reason to apologize to the wolf who is denied his leg of lamb? Certain philosophers would answer that question: yes. Something important is lost, they say, whenever people of extraordinary spirit and ambition are thwarted by the laws of moral pygmies. I'm not asking whether anyone could think that. I'm asking what you think. And if you, like me, think that nothing wrong is done through such laws, then you will have that reason for rejecting Berlin's account of liberty. If his view that a conflict between liberty and equality is inevitable depends on that account of liberty, then you will have that reason for rejecting that view as well.

Of course I have not shown that conflicts between liberty and equality are not inevitable. Perhaps there is a more subtle account of liberty than Berlin's, which is not open to the objection I made, but which would still guarantee conflicts between liberty and equality. My point has been a limited one. I have tried, first, to clarify Berlin's important thesis about value pluralism, to show its originality, interest and ambition, and, second, to show how difficult it is to sustain that ambitious thesis. Berlin said that the value conflicts he described were all about us, and evident to all except the immature. I do not think that he sustained that very broad claim; indeed, as I have just argued, I do not think he sustained it even in the case he took as paradigm: the supposed conflict between liberty and equality.

That does not mean the defeat of value pluralism. But it does suggest, I believe, that the argument necessary to defend pluralism must be a very long and complex one. That argument must show, in the case of each of the values it takes to be in some kind of conceptual conflict with one another, why the understanding of that value that produces the conflict is the most appropriate one. Nothing is easier than composing definitions of liberty, equality, democracy, community and justice that conflict with one another. But not much, in philosophy, is harder than showing why these are the definitions that we should accept. There is no short cut to that demonstration. Perhaps, after all, the most attractive conceptions of the leading liberal values do hang together in the right way. We haven't yet been given reason to abandon that hope.

BERNARD WILLIAMS

Liberalism and Loss

ALTHOUGH, AS RONALD Dworkin said, the idea of
"value pluralism" goes more widely, I am going to talk
primarily about politics. If you will permit me, I would
like to take a few minutes in setting out a structure
which I think helps to make sense of the idea. Isaiah
himself did not explicitly set it out in these terms,
though the kind of structure I have in mind is, I am
sure, implicit in a good deal of what he did say about
these matters.

I start from what seems to me a very important
remark of Nietzsche's (a thinker for whom Isaiah himself was not a great enthusiast), who said, "The only
things that are definable are those that have no history." This seems to me profoundly true. The values
that we are concerned with here—values such as liberty, equality, and justice—all have a very significant
history, and that history stands in the way of their simply having a definition. (This, incidentally, is why,
when Isaiah used to say that in studying such concepts
he had turned from philosophy to the history of ideas,
he did not state his own position quite accurately.

Rather, he turned from a form of philosophy which ignored history to a form of philosophy which did not ignore history.)

I agree entirely with Ronald Dworkin that the identification of concepts such as liberty and justice is a problematic and difficult matter. In fact, my own view is that the question of how we should think about the identity and the structure of such concepts is one that philosophy has scarcely even addressed: people have not thought in a very productive way about the ways in which such concepts should be identified, and the ways in which their structure must contribute to this. But let us take a kind of sketch that seems to be promising, a sketch that indeed fits in with Isaiah's ideas.

The first thing we have to bear in mind is that liberty and equality—let us say, rather more broadly, liberty and justice—are two *different* values. Even Ronald Dworkin does not deny this: these two are not simply different names for the same concept. That is an important fact, and there must be some way of understanding it. One way of looking at it is in terms of our concern for such values, what it is that we care about in these connections. It is reasonable to think that associated with each such value concept there is a kind of schema, a very bare outline of what our central concern is. For instance, in the case of liberty, it might be that the concern was not to be in somebody else's power. In the case of justice, it might be that of giving each person what he or she should have, or some similar idea.

Incidentally, I did not suggest that the schema or matrix of liberty might be found in Isaiah's definition of negative liberty, and it is important that the idea of pluralism is in no way essentially connected with that definition of liberty. It is a more general notion, which may be better expressed in terms of some other account of liberty. In fact, I agree with Ronald Dworkin that somebody who thought that liberty *as a political value* had been sacrificed when one person was stopped by the law from murdering another would be off the rails. He should recognize that no concept of liberty intelligible as a political value could allow anybody to murder anybody they liked. A prohibition or limitation on that kind of thing is a necessary condition of there being any politics or political values at all.

The schema or matrix attached to a given value concept is not going to achieve much by itself: it is too bare, indeed too schematic. It needs, and will have indeed received, an associated social, historical, and cultural elaboration. The idea of not being in somebody else's power, say, or that of giving each what he should have, may well be simply in themselves something like human universals, but equally they are very indeterminate; how they determinately work out in different contexts, in different cultures, in different societies, is something that will require a historical story.

But now we have a further fact about these concepts, that they carry evaluations about which some people care a lot, and they impact on people's interests in ways that everyone cares about a great deal. This is intelligible in terms of the matrix: for instance, it is a plausible guess at a human universal that people resent being, as they see it, arbitrarily pushed around by others. What counts as "arbitrary" and so on—these are the matters of historical and social elaboration which make the value in question locally intelligible.

Let us call these two things together—the basic schema of concern, and a given historical elaboration or application of it—the *contour* of the value in a given society or historical situation. When we consider what is involved in there being such a thing, we reach a conclusion which (it seems to me) is very important, that the concerns which basically go with these various values cannot be redirected simply nominalistically, by redefining a word. Suppose that somebody produces a definition or understanding of liberty, and a definition or understanding of justice, and then for systematic reasons tries to make the two values fit together, in the strong sense that they will be immune to certain kinds of principled conflict. He does not claim merely that this would be theoretically tidier and simpler: it would, he says, reduce political and legal conflict and altogether would make more sense of our situation if we defined the terms in this way. He may indeed have some reason to say this. But the significant point is that you cannot necessarily get the basic concerns that go with those values to follow these systematic proposals, because the *concern* with the value is directed to the thing that was picked out in the matrix, which in turn is mediated by the history. An interest in producing a more coherent body of law is not by itself going to stop the concern going to what the concern goes to. What will matter is the relation or analogy that some new proposed application or extension of the value bears to the schema as it has been expressed in the historical structure—that is to say, to what I have called "the contour."

Granted some such account—and I have obviously only gestured to it in the time available to us—it is obvious that there is no particular reason why the respective contours of two such concepts, the focus of concern in this historically mediated way, should not conflict and lead to a sense of loss. In fact, granted the political and social realities which such concepts try to address, there is every reason to think that they may do so. Of course it does not follow that they always will conflict, but what does follow is the permanent possibility of conflict, and this is implicit in the structure of these concepts as values. In that sense, it is, as Isaiah said it was, a conceptual truth that values will conflict.

The reasons why there will be conflict operate on at least two different levels. First, there is a special reason why there should be conflict in societies, such as our own, which display a high level of social pluralism. The reason why there are potential conflicts here is that the contour of a given value is not the same for all parties in the society. That is, the historical and cultural interpretation of the matrix, and perhaps, to some degree, the conception of the matrix itself, differ between them, for reasons which have indeed a hermeneutical or historical explanation. We can explain why what looks like liberty and what looks like justice to one group of people who have an identifiable and intelligible cultural history, should be somewhat different from what counts as liberty and justice with some other group in the same society.

The fact that this can be a matter of historical or hermeneutical understanding is entirely consistent with its being at the same time a matter of practical concern, and this is one reason why the unity of history and philosophy in Isaiah's political outlook need not imply a spectatorial conservatism. One way of interpreting the value of, say, freedom, makes sense to us, and a slightly different one makes sense to these other people. In addition, it makes sense to us that that other way of looking at freedom should make sense to them. This does not mean that we have nothing to say about this difference between ourselves and them. On the contrary, our understanding of our and their situation itself gives us things to say, things relevant to our explaining why we think our ideas fit the situation better than theirs do—a situation which, under some description or other, we indisputably both share. (Of course, just in virtue of understanding how they and we come to be where we respectively are, we might well be amazed if we could get them to agree with us.)

Even if we waive local pluralism, and assume a society which is less pluralistic than ours, it is still going to be true that the basic interest in liberty and the basic interest in justice as mediated through their historical realizations may be such that the given resolution of a dispute which is positive in virtue of the contour of justice is negative in virtue of the contour of liberty, or the converse. Of course, once again, it is not always so. If it were, the system would be exceedingly conflictual, which I want to emphasize in this context is to be seen as a political and ethical disadvantage, not a purely intellectual or systematic one.

So there is no reason to expect these concepts of value to be exempt from the kinds of conflict that are associated with other ideas that people care about, conflicts which Ronald Dworkin indeed acknowledges. It might be the case that for reasons of justice or liberty or the preservation of property rights or something, we were not able, for instance, to preserve some very beautiful building. This would be an occasion for regret and sadness, and Ronald Dworkin does not want to deny this. He acknowledges the existence of painful, even tragic, choices. I take his point to be this: that while with cases that involve liberty and justice there can be apparent conflict and room for regret, liberty and justice cannot really conflict if they are correctly understood: and what this means is that if the apparent conflict is correctly resolved, nobody will have been wronged. This is what creates the cutting edge of his opposition to pluralism: the insistence that if you get the definitions of liberty and equality right, then even though there may be seeming conflict and a sense of loss, nobody will have been wronged.

I do not want to deny this, in a certain sense of "being wronged." However, everything turns on what that sense is and what kinds of loss there are. Ronald Dworkin's particular stance represents a very sharp articulation of resistance to value pluralism, but its basis, I think (and he will recognize this criticism), is that he models political decisions that involve principle—as opposed to those that merely involve interests—on the pattern of decisions of constitutional law. Moreover, decisions of constitutional law are themselves understood in such a way that, first, if the case is rightly decided, no one will have been wronged; and, second, the only complaint about the decision that could carry any real or ultimate ethical weight would be a complaint that someone had been wronged.

Of course the resolution of any conflict, except in the most favorable circumstances, will issue in disappointment and regret for someone. We all recognize this, as Ronald Dworkin reminds us, when it takes the form of interests, and this extends in a familiar way beyond merely material interests, and beyond a merely personal concern. Something you would like to have happened didn't happen. One of your friends hasn't prospered as well as one of your friends might have done. Something to which you attached some cultural value has been sacrificed. It does not follow that you or anyone else has been wronged. The crucial questions I want to put to Ronald Dworkin are these: what exactly is the force of this consideration, whether someone has been wronged, and does he think that this is the only consideration in these connections that (really, ultimately) matters?

I'm not going to discuss the issue of how far those two claims—that if a conflict of principle has been decided rightly then no one has been wronged, and that (as I am putting it) the only thing that matters is whether someone is wronged—are indeed correct about decisions of constitutional law. Maybe they are

correct about decisions of constitutional law, but I
think the fundamental error is to suppose that decisions of politics, even those that involve issues of principle, are in such ways like decisions of constitutional
law. Let us go back to the situation in a society which
is itself pluralistic. Take a situation in which some people think that the wrong political decision was made,
because they have rather different conceptions of liberty and justice from those that prevailed in the decision. They think that the matter should have been
decided otherwise. These people need not necessarily
think that the losing party (say, themselves) has been
wronged in terms of the actual process, because they
know they are a minority in a pluralistic state and given
the actual situation, they have no complaint about the
way the decision was made. But they do have a complaint about what came out of it: this is not a complaint
of being wronged, but it certainly is not just a complaint to the effect that their interests have lost out.
Their conception of liberty, liberty as they conceive it,
has been violated in virtue of a certain conception of
justice which they do not share. They have a complaint
in liberty even though they do not think that they were
wronged.

Somebody may say, does it matter whether we talk
about being wronged, or exactly how we use these normative conceptions? We might just compromise. Ronald
Dworkin and I can say, "Well, let's agree that in some
cases when you do what is just, something will have
been done that is bad or regrettable from the point of
view of liberty. It doesn't mean you were wrong. It

doesn't mean you ought to have done something else, but it was to that extent a bad thing." Well, we could spend—indeed, he and I have spent—a good deal of time in juggling such options. But I think all those options are secondary to an important question. *What is it that you say to the people who have the complaint?* What he tells them is the same thing as Rousseau told them, that they did not really understand what liberty was.

Take a case. A radical administration in some country which does not have a constitutional court wants in the name of social justice to advance equality of opportunity in school education. It rightly believes that the existence of a large sector of private fee-paying education stands in the way of this (the wealthier classes are not really interested in state schools, and so on). The government takes steps to make it illegal or effectively impossible, except for some fairly trivial exceptions, to run a private school. Objectors complain that their own and others' liberty (and they do not simply mean by this their interests, or their power to do what they like) has been restricted by this pursuit of equality. They are told that it is in the interests of justice and equality, and they might even agree that it was in the interests of justice and equality, that their children should not go to private schools, but they nevertheless think that stopping them doing so is a limitation of their liberty, and they have the feelings that people have when such things are done to them, such as resentment.

Isaiah said to them, "You are right—there was a cost in liberty, but no one can have everything. The democratically elected government is advancing equality and social justice, and those values may well be advanced by this, but there is a cost in liberty." What would Ronald Dworkin say to them? As a matter of fact, I have reason to think that he would support the objectors on this particular question, and he would not accept that the government's measures would be just. So let us imagine someone else, call him Jean-Jacques, who shares his opposition to pluralism but supports this government's policy. Jean-Jacques says to the objectors, "You only think that you have a complaint in liberty because you haven't understood what liberty is. If you really understood what liberty is, you would know that it is consistent with social justice, and so with equality. Being prevented from sending your children to private schools is not, as you falsely suppose, a limitation of your liberty. It is actually a way of advancing liberty, when you understand what liberty truly is."

Now I don't think that this is the best thing to say to these people. I don't think that it assists them in being citizens or us in living together with them, in most cases. This is because politics is neither morality nor constitutional law. Of course, everyone agrees to this in general; what may be less well understood is that the politics of principle isn't morality or constitutional law either.

I suspect that in these mistaken conceptions of politics there is lurking a Kantian dualism, to the effect that there is one world of interests which consists of winning and losing, and another world of principle, which is expressed in being right or wrong. What Isaiah insisted on was that a decision which is not a mere matter of interests can involve a loss in the dimension of a certain value. That is, people can appropriately have something like the reactions that are appropriate to a violation of the contour of that value, without necessarily thinking that the decision was, in the circumstances, the wrong decision, nor that it involved anyone's being wronged.

It seems to me a very desirable feature of a civil society, particularly a pluralistic society, that citizens and politicians should understand this. Politics provides a dimension which can be governed by values as well as by interests, and to that extent it is a principled space, but one in which a decision going against you does not have to mean that you were wrong. It may merely mean that you lost. That is what politics is about. Telling these people that they had better wise up and revise their definition of the values involved is not in many cases prudent, or citizenly, or respectful of their experience. Moreover, to pick up a political point that Ronald Dworkin made at the beginning of his remarks, it is not necessarily the best way of getting them to accept more radical policies. The idea of value pluralism is not that of an inert spectatorial conservatism; it can indeed be used in the interests of an inert spectatorial conservatism, an aestheticism of politics, but that is not what it is. Rather, it tells you how to speak to the people who have to pay, not just in their interests but in their values, for things that have to be done. That is a form of citizenly address, particularly in a pluralistic society.

When it is and when it is not appropriate to go further and say, "You've got the idea of liberty wrong"— and it is sometimes appropriate—that itself is a matter not just of philosophical, but of political judgment. All this, as a matter of biographical fact, I think Isaiah believed, and that is why he believed in pluralism. That is why he thought that a proper understanding of pluralism was central to a tolerant, unfanatical and honest liberal society.

THOMAS NAGEL

Pluralism and Coherence

MY DISCUSSION WILL approach the subject of pluralism through ethical theory rather than politics or history, but I will make some remarks about political theory at the end.

In spite of the importance that we have seen throughout the conference so far of the connection in Isaiah Berlin's thought between values and history, he was not a historicist about value. He was, I would say, a moral realist. What makes his pluralism so unusual and philosophically interesting is, as Ronald Dworkin said, that it is a realistic pluralism, not a relativistic one. Berlin insisted on this: he believed that there were real, noncontingently conflicting values.

Of course he believed these values were developed and discovered and understood through historical traditions, but they were not just the attitudes of particular groups or individuals. They were real values that provided real reasons for action, and the conflicts to which they gave rise were therefore extremely troubling. So value pluralism was not just a psychological matter for Berlin. Nor was it only because of limitations in resources or other practical difficulties that there were conflicts between values. He maintained that in many cases values can conflict noncontingently or essentially.

One can distinguish two types of noncontingent conflict between values, both of which Berlin pointed out, and which I will call incompatibility and opposition. (Opposition might also be thought of as a kind of contradiction.)

By "incompatibility" I mean the impossibility in principle of realizing one value while realizing the other, or without frustrating the other. Berlin likened this to the incompatibility between musical or artistic styles. In individual life there are many conflicts of value that are examples of incompatibility. One can't lead both a rural and an urban life, or a life of hard physical exertion and of intellectual contemplation. These incompatibilities do not, I think, present a profound problem for moral theory, though they may present us with difficult choices. There are many goods, and there is not enough space in any one life for more than a limited number of them. Exactly the same problem arises in the case of limited social space. There are alternative good societies that realize to different degrees the disparate values of order, respect for tradition, social mobility, individualism, public beauty, commercial variety, technological progress, preservation of nature and so forth. These values in many cases clash with one another noncontingently, not just because of the limitation of resources, but because their realizations are to some degree incompatible.

The more difficult case is the case of a true opposition between values, which arises when each value actually condemns the other, rather than merely inter-fering with it. This is the nature of the specific example of value conflict that Berlin cites as having given him his original pluralistic insight: namely the conflict, pointed out by Machiavelli, between the virtues of Christian humility and the pagan virtues of assertion and power. Each of these is a genuine value, and each of them is not only incompatible in its realization with the other, but actually condemns the other as contrary to virtue and therefore to be avoided. There are other examples, many of them from among the virtues and values of individual life and conduct: hedonism versus asceticism, self-control versus spontaneity, worldliness versus spirituality, individualism versus communitari-anism, outspokenness versus tact. Though they are opposed to one another, we can recognize most of these things as good and as defining forms of value that one might well pursue. But each of them to one degree or another essentially condemns its rival.

All of these oppositions could, perhaps, be toned down to mere incompatibilities, so that they don't actu-ally condemn each other: they could be turned into more tolerant values, so to speak. But I think that Berlin believed, rightly, that some of them were in direct and irresolvable opposition. I am not sure where the oppo-sition between liberty and equality falls on Berlin's view. I suspect that it would count as an incompatibility rather than as a direct essential opposition. But in either case the conflict between them is certainly contrary to the view that Ronald Dworkin expressed, which attempts to transcend the opposition by an interpretation or reinterpretation of liberty and equality, which would make them fit together without conflict.

Like Bernard Williams, I am somewhat skeptical about Dworkin's proposal to solve this problem by introducing the conception of liberty as doing what you like with what is rightfully yours, because I think the problem will just arise again. That is, the conflict between the values of liberty and equality will arise again in any answer to the question, "What is rightfully yours?"

The main philosophical point of Berlin's position is that the logic of values differs from the logic of facts. On his view, although not on everyone's view—but certainly on mine also—truth in science, in mathematics, or in history has to fit together in a consistent system. We may not actually have a consistent system of beliefs about one or another of these domains. But if we find good reasons to believe two things that turn out to contradict one another, that gives us a task, which it may be impossible to carry out successfully, of looking for a solution which removes the inconsistency. We have either to modify or to abandon one or the other of the beliefs. We can perhaps deal with the problem by reinterpreting them relativistically or subjectively, but we've got to do something in order to allow a single world to be described by the total collection of our factual beliefs.

Berlin thought, however, that in the case of value we should accept as final, or certainly could accept as final, certain essential noncontingent conflicts between values. He also thought, I believe, that even in many cases of incompatibilities between values—where there was unavoidable competition over which of them could be realized—there was no higher vantage point of evaluation from which we could make the right choice between them, or even from which we could say that they were evenly balanced so that it was all right to make either choice.

Now I believe that as a matter of logic this is possible. Our evaluative beliefs are not part of the attempt to describe a single world, as our historical or scientific beliefs are. There may be real nonsubjective values that provide only a partial normative ordering of possibilities in life, or of choices among social systems. I think that it can even be the case that in some respects real values will yield mutually inconsistent orderings, leading to conflicts between individuals who justify their choices and order their lives or their societies by reference to these conflicting values.

But as a matter of substantive judgment I think that Berlin was too pessimistic about the possibility and desirability of searching for a level of evaluation that would bring into being greater consistency out of this pluralism—not in the way of the description of a single world, as in the factual domain, but rather through the development of some form of accommodation that could be claimed to be more or less objectively correct, in the same sense that the values in the pluralistic mix were themselves correct.

One doesn't have to give up pluralism in order to accept this aim of overcoming or at least reducing value conflict. One of the important things about Berlin's

pluralism is that he urged us always to resist reductionist solutions to it—to continue to recognize the reality
of the conflicting values that give us this task. But it
seems to me that the pressures toward the discovery of
a coherent solution remain strong when different people invoke different values. The source of that pressure
is the search for common methods of justification, so
that we can think of ourselves as living in a common
moral universe with those with whom we interact. And
of course these pressures are strongest when we interact through political institutions.

There is no guarantee of reaching acceptable results,
but the pressures toward objectivity and a right answer,
even on a base of conflicting pluralistic values, are very
strong wherever values come into practical conflict. The
aim should not be to deny pluralism but to encompass
it in a system that permits conflicts to be adjudicated
without the triumph of one master value over its rivals.

This, I think, is the core of liberalism in political
theory. Therefore I don't think that liberalism is particularly supported by the most radical form of opposi-
tional pluralism that Berlin has been associated with.
In order to provide a pluralistic defense of political liberalism it would be sufficient to deny that the plurality
of conflicting values could be eliminated by reducing
them all to a common denominator, but nevertheless to
maintain that the search for higher-order values, or for
methods that permit the conflicts to be resolved, is a
reasonable one.

Finally, to make the connection to history, I believe
that the proper attitude toward this enterprise is to

think of ourselves as participants in a historical development that is in process of giving rise to the values that we can hope will prevail in the future. We should think of ourselves as responding to the multiplicity of values that historical traditions have presented us with, and should try to take the next step under the pressure of the search for coherence.

CHARLES TAYLOR

Plurality of Goods

ISAIAH BERLIN'S BEST-KNOWN philosophical thesis, perhaps apart from the positive/negative freedom distinction, is the idea that we find ourselves drawn to a plurality of goods, some of which are incompatible.

This thesis supposes some kind of moral realism, or cognitivism; that is, it supposes that I see these goods as in some way imposing themselves, as binding on me, or making a claim on me. Otherwise the conflict could be easily set aside. Or at least, the conflict would turn out to be one in me, something that I could straighten out if I could just achieve some harmony in my goals.

The reason why this may need to be said is that Isaiah also noted another, quite different kind of value pluralism, which sometimes at least encourages a non-cognitivist or anti-realist view. Just because he explored with such sympathy and such insight rather different historically held outlooks, Isaiah's work pointed up how diverse these outlooks are. Human beings in the course of history have espoused a tremendous range of value positions, and of course the values of this whole range aren't combinable. That is hardly news. But this variety sometimes encourages us to adopt a non-cognitivist position, not only because that offers an easy way of explaining the fact of difference, but also because the alternative seems to be to hold that we are right and those others are wrong, and this seems arrogant, Western-chauvinist, or politically incorrect.

But the value pluralism for which Isaiah is famous is not this historical or cross-cultural one, but rather the view that among the goods which we cannot help but recognize, if we are honest and sincere with ourselves, there are often, even perhaps always, incompatibilities which require that we make hard choices, foregoing some for others, or foregoing each to some degree.

If we are honest and sincere... This is an important clause, because Isaiah thought that we have strong temptations to fudge or cover up on this issue. One of the crucial points of "Two Concepts of Liberty" was just this: we try to finesse the clash between liberty and some other goal—solidarity, justice, social harmony, equality—by telling ourselves that these other goals are internal to the definition of freedom, properly understood. Thus the forms of liberty which seem to clash with them aren't true forms. They don't need to be defended. *Real* liberty incorporates solidarity, or whatever. Hence we are justified in compelling people if they try to act on a form of liberty which clashes with this other good; this compulsion is not suppressing freedom, not *real* freedom.

"Two Concepts" was written to protest against this dishonest sleight of hand. This is the burden of the attack against most doctrines of "positive freedom."

We might recognize them as valid if they were presented as affirming other, independent goods, which might be in conflict with negative freedom, and thus would force us to take difficult choices. But as doctrines of *real* freedom, they were a hoax.

This kind of fudging goes back to Plato, at least. It is central to his doctrine in the *Republic* that all virtues go together, they are all born of the same condition, of love of wisdom and the unchanging. The idea that you might have some without others, even that in certain conditions, the full development of some might militate against that of others, is utterly rejected. This means that the virtues have to be reconceptualized. They are in a sense all intellectualized, aligned with wisdom as the central one. Thus courage is defined as the right opinion concerning what is really to be feared and so on. The courageous person has his priorities right; he knows that eternal dishonor is more to be feared than death on the battlefield, and thus stands his ground. Conflict is finessed by redefinition, as with the doctrines of positive liberty.

These maneuvers lack intellectual honesty in the last analysis, or so one could judge them if one took the harsh view that Isaiah does in "Two Concepts." But we can also see them as lacking in sincerity, if this is the right term; as exhibiting a failure to acknowledge to oneself some of the goods which one can't help valuing deep down. The militant who forces the recalcitrant "bourgeois" into line still really values negative freedom for himself, and he discovers this, too late, when the apparatus turns on him and sends him to the

Gulag. Rare is the fanatic who can consistently will his own destruction in conformity with the ideology he espouses. Most people who espouse these modes of positive liberty naively assume deep down that all good things fit together as the doctrine promises, e.g., that Communism also means maximum negative liberty, once we get rid of all those scheming enemies of the working class.

And in fact, the most influential modern doctrines of the compatibility of the good don't depend on these tendentious redefinitions, but rather on the exclusion of a number of goods, either from consideration altogether, or from the "top table." That is, they are not "moral" goods. They can be pursued, but they have lower priorities.

The most influential modern moral theories, at least in the Anglo-Saxon world, utilitarianism and Kantianism, operate this kind of pre-shrinking of the moral domain. The gain is a system in which all obligatory actions can be derived from a single principle (although they disagree radically on the principle). The attraction of this is partly its rationalism: morality can be founded on clear, unambiguous reasoning. But it also has the incidental result of avoiding a clash of goods. On any one issue we have only one obligation, that which the calculation or reasoning identifies, and so there cannot be agonizing dilemmas.

But, of course, this means pitching overboard a great many of the goods we recognize. Utilitarianism has no place for rights (although there is often an attempt to recapture exactly the same results in utility terms, another example of the deplorable fudging which bad meta-ethical theories encourage), or for virtues, conceptions of the good life. Kantianism is well placed on the rights front, but is forced to put conceptions of the good life in another category, as we see with Habermas.

Isaiah's plurality thesis was not only a blow to various totalitarian theories of positive liberty, it was also deeply unsettling to the moral theories dominant in his own milieu. It is one of the paradoxes of our intellec tual world, which will be increasingly discussed in the future, why this latter point was not realized. The bomb was planted in the academy, but somehow failed to go off. In part, this was due to its packaging. Just because Isaiah said to all and sundry that he had more or less "emigrated" from philosophy, his colleagues felt that their own systems were not targeted in his remarks. But the challenge seems evident once you set aside these irrelevant disciplinary labels.

For those of us who don't accept the artificial barriers and distinctions of modern moral theory, Isaiah's work is an important statement.

If I have a criticism, it is that he seems to have stated the conflict of goods as though it were written into the goods themselves. Whereas I think it arises from the complexity and limitations of human life. We can be virtually certain that we shall always face such conflicts, just as we can be certain that there will always be some conflict and bad feeling between different groups of human beings; in each case, the human condition contains such varied grounds for opposition that it would be a virtual miracle were they to be absent altogether.

But that doesn't mean that the opposition is fated in any given case, either between goods or between groups. It always makes sense to work toward a condition in which two cherished goods can be combined, or at least traded off at a higher level, just as it does to work for peace between any pair of combatants. Such adjudication and balance are possible if we approach value pluralism in an Aristotelian framework. That is, in any given situation we can weigh the relative importance of the goods that concern us, in some cases upholding one more strongly, and in others another. We can, in effect, trade goods off against one another. We see this for example in Tocqueville's effort to balance equality and democracy against the excellent, exceptional, and heroic. And it's quite possible that in any given circumstance the overwhelming weight of one good will clearly take precedence against the lesser weight of another. In a conflict between freedom and the public good, for example, in any given case it may be that the freedom in question is trivial and the public good significant. Or the opposite may be true. Or the demands of these goods may be so balanced that we find it difficult to agree. But in principle we can apply this approach to defend one good against another in a given situation.

It may also be that what appears as an opposition between goods at one stage of history is seen merely as an incompatibility at a later stage, and that even the incompatibilities may sometimes be overcome. In the eighteenth century, many people feared democracy for its potential destructive effects on public order. And in many cases they weren't wrong then. Today, democratic societies in general enjoy the highest degree of internal peace and order. But it took the development of new political cultures for this happy state of affairs to come about. And of course, these cultures perhaps involve certain disciplines which are inhibiting other goods. New conflicts emerge in the course of resolving old ones. But no particular one need be considered immovable. We don't have merely to resign ourselves.

And sometimes new values emerge. For example, the goal of "authenticity," developing out of the Herderian idea that each person has his own way of being, is genuinely new. It was not part of the philosophical vocabulary of the seventeenth century, or for that matter of ancient Greece or the Middle Ages.

Again, to take a contemporary example, the demands for male-female equality, and the re-ordering of social, sexual and family life, have in some cases deeply upset the process of forming gender identities; some of the old landmarks for these identities have been swept away. This generates conflict, alienation, a lot of suffering. But there is no reason to take this as the last word on the subject; new identity-modes are being explored. We can work to reconcile the goods here. But for this it helps greatly to have a theory which allows us to acknowledge the conflicts. For this we can thank Isaiah.

DISCUSSION

Pluralism

RONALD DWORKIN: Bernard Williams, with characteristic acumen, points to the pivotal issue in my argument. I concede, as Bernard says, that a political community cannot have everything it wants or even everything it should want. A war on poverty, as he says, will almost always mean less money for the arts. But so long as I concede conflicts of that kind, have I not conceded Berlin's point?

I don't think so. Berlin had in mind grave conflicts, the kind that, as he put it, inevitably produce "irreparable loss." His emphasis on the supposed conflict between liberty and equality make that plain. We appeal to distinct political values, like liberty and equality, to describe what we take to be not merely citizens' interests but their rights, and we agree that violating a citizen's rights doesn't merely disappoint him but wrongs him. On occasion a state might be justified in overriding such a right, in virtue of some special emergency, but even then the wrong remains—the state's action, though justified, leaves what some philosophers call a moral "residue"—and it is therefore appropriate for the state to show remorse, to apologize, and even, when this is feasible, to make amends or compensation. That is why arguments about liberty and equality are politically so important. If conservatives said only that the rich don't want to pay taxes, or are disappointed and unhappy when they are made to do so, their claim would have only limited importance. But when they claim that taxation invades liberty, they have raised the stakes, and it becomes crucial to decide whether they are right.

Berlin's value pluralism would be unremarkable, as I said, if he meant only that sometimes a state must disappoint some of its citizens. His claim is important because he insists that some citizens' rights to liberty conflict with other citizens' rights to equality, so that the government must not merely disappoint but must wrong some citizens no matter what it does. I tried to test that claim using the admittedly crude example of murder. On Berlin's account of liberty, government wrongs would-be murderers to some degree when it thwarts them, even though it is overall justified in doing so. If, as I suggested, that makes no sense, then Berlin's account of liberty is unsuccessful, and provides no basis for his claim that political rights conflict in a way that produces irreparable loss no matter what government does.

I understand why Bernard refers to my interest in constitutional law. When the Supreme Court decided —wrongly as almost everyone now thinks—that the government had the constitutional power to intern Americans of Japanese descent at the start of World War II, it decided that the government had done no legal wrong to them, and Bernard worries that all that I mean, when I suggest that perhaps liberty and equality do not conflict after all, is that government need not do any legal wrong to anyone when it prefers one of these values to the other. But that is not what I mean. I assume that even the justices who upheld the internment as necessary would have agreed that those interned had nevertheless been wronged. When I suggest that liberty and equality do not necessarily conflict, I am suggesting, not simply that government need not violate the Constitution to protect equality, but that it need not violate liberty on any defensible conception of what liberty is.

I want to comment, finally, on the role that the other panelists have assigned to history. We must take care to distinguish three issues. What have people argued and divided about in the past? How can people be brought to argue and divide less now? When they do argue and divide, is one side right and, if so, which side? Berlin spoke to all three of these questions, but one of his great contributions was to distinguish them, and his remarks about value pluralism were addressed to the third. In what way does history help us to get clearer about that question? For example: when is it right that some people be in each other's power and when not? Bernard says history shows us that people have a great desire not to be in anybody else's power, and that our concern with liberty stems from that concern. But he also says that sometimes it is no violation of liberty when some people are in other people's power. The murderer ought to be in our power, says Bernard, and it would be silly to think this was an invasion of his liberty.

So we need something more than history here. We need to confront the essentially moral question of how to construe the ideal of liberty. We may find—indeed we are almost certain to find—that people disagree about that question and that some people, even after the most cordial and complete discussion, continue to embrace an account of liberty according to which, for example, taxation compromises liberty. What shall we say to them?

We might be tempted to say, as a matter of courtesy or strategy, that they are right, that our taxes have compromised their freedom, but that since values necessarily conflict some compromise of some value is necessary, and that we have chosen to prefer equality to liberty, at least on this occasion. But I think that it is better to say to them (if that is what we think) that they are wrong about what liberty is, and that on the better conception, taxation does not compromise liberty at all. We might well add that we know that their view of liberty has an important historical pedigree, that their opinion is not stupid or contemptible. We need not pick a fight or insult them. But we must offer an honest explanation of why we have rejected their demands, and any honest explanation must include the fact that we think they are mistaken about liberty.

Value pluralism, it seems to me, is too often cited as a kind of excuse for not confronting the most fundamental substantive issues: it is easier to say that our values conflict, and that the majority has simply chosen one set while knowing that the minority, with equal justification, might well have chosen another, than it is

to do the hard work of actually trying to identify the
right conceptions of the values in question. But we owe
ourselves, as well as those who disagree with us, a more
honest effort and accounting.

BERNARD WILLIAMS: Well, we've obviously got to get
clear what we are disagreeing about. I do think it matters what you say to people in these circumstances, but
of course you are right, that isn't itself the question. It
is a question of how the view you take of these matters
plays out in terms of what you say to other people.
Now, you agree that situations are possible, where, as
the pluralists would put it, one value is asserted with
the result of the loss of or damage to or sacrifice of
something else. The losing party may lose with respect
to his interests. There may be regret. There may be various sorts of sense of loss. There may even be radical
damage to some people—you do not adopt the position that the only thing that could really ever harm
someone was wronging him.

MR. DWORKIN: I do not, no.

MR. WILLIAMS: So all of these things are possible. The
question is therefore, what is it that in rejecting value
pluralism you think is impossible? I thought that, in
rejecting value pluralism, you held that there was some
very important sense of "affirming one value at the
cost of sacrificing another" in which it is impossible to
do such a thing. That is to say, that if we understand
the two values correctly, we cannot agree that one of

them was properly asserted "with the sacrifice of the other." Now you've agreed to all the other things that might happen. So what I have to ask you still is: what is the sense of the "sacrifice" of a value such that you think that when values are properly understood, it can never be the case that in rightfully asserting one of them, we sacrifice the other?

If that isn't important, if there is not some basic impossibility here, then it seems to me that we simply are left with a perfectly manageable discussion about how much time you spend on redefining values, how much time you spend in apologizing, how much time you spend trying to do other things within the compass of the sort of liberal de Tocquevillian program which Charles Taylor quite properly put before us. Do you think there is a sense in which, if values are properly understood, then it cannot be the case that one of them rightfully asserted leads to the sacrifice of the other?

MR. DWORKIN: I haven't made that strong a claim. I've said that we should concentrate on finding the most attractive conceptions of our political values, and only then ask whether, on those attractive conceptions, these values conflict. But, as I said, "finding" the most attractive conception isn't a matter of excavating the shared meanings of words or of anything like a scientific discovery about the true nature of reality. We construct conceptions of our values, trying to refine the initial abstract impressions and agreements I mentioned into more precise accounts of the values we believe at stake in our arguments.

I've been concentrating so far on a negative claim about that process: that we have been given no reason for thinking, in advance, that when we construct these conceptions with that aim in view we will encounter conflicts of the kind Berlin declared, that is, not merely conflicts in interests but conflicts that mean that, whatever we do, we do wrong. In particular, Berlin's remarks about liberty and equality fail to show this, for the reasons I suggested. I see no reason yet to think that we can't fight our way to attractive conceptions that capture what we actually value and that do not produce conflicts of the kind Berlin thought pervasive.

But now a more positive claim. It seems to me that integrity among our concepts is itself a value, so that we have that standing reason for seeking out, for preferring, conceptions of our values that do not conflict. It doesn't follow, of course, that we will succeed, because our accounts of the various values must make sense to us in their own terms—our theory of liberty won't work, that is, unless it matches our reflective convictions about what counts as a wrongful deprivation of freedom. We might find that we cannot respect our convictions and have integrity too. In that case, we would have to concede conflict. But I think we have a pretty good shot at having them both, and we should aim in that direction.

For purposes of this discussion, however, it's the negative claim I've been trying to emphasize. In this I think I'm speaking in the same spirit as Thomas Nagel and Charles Taylor. We shouldn't buy failure in advance: we should aim at integrity in an optimistic spirit. Nice goal if you can get it.

MARK LILLA: I wonder if I can turn the discussion a little more back to Berlin and his own interest in laying out this notion of value pluralism. I think his concern was not the conflict among political values, but the conflict between political values and nonpolitical values. Hence his extensive writings about the natural and social sciences and what happens to literature and poetry under totalitarianism. What revolted him about what the Soviet Union was willing to do to Anna Akhmatova was not only that it was willing to rob an individual of her liberty, but that some other line had also been crossed. What repelled him was any unwillingness to recognize a distinction between political values and other things, which he believed could not be compared or traded off in a way that leaves us morally indifferent. One of Isaiah's least favorite Russian novelists, Dostoyevsky, has a character in *Crime and Punishment* say, "Which is more valuable, Shakespeare or a pair of boots?" That question, I submit, is coursing throughout his works. And I'm wondering, Ronald Dworkin, if you think that the problem is just as soluble when we get to Shakespeare and boots as it is when we talk about liberty and equality.

MR. DWORKIN: Political theory is very broad: it's about how the state's monopoly of power should be used. So anything can come into the discussion, including Shakespeare and boots. When you say that sometimes it is wrong to sacrifice the personal values of individuals to an overall political goal, you're raising a political issue. Are personal and political values in some way incommensurate so that you can't suppose that one could override or extinguish the other? That is itself a moral issue. Some reductionist political theories—utilitarianism, for example—say that all values are commensurate. Others deny this. Am I missing the point of the question?

MR. LILLA: But aren't you begging the question when you take precisely the political point of view to this problem? From the point of view of poetry, the issue is not how we come to a social decision about the value of poetry, or how much of it we need.

MR. DWORKIN: But I'm not leaving anything out by saying that there might be an issue of political morality raised by asking whether Shakespeare is more important than boots. Of course we can ask many questions about the value of poetry that aren't political. There are many fora in which we can debate whether poetry is more or less important than making sure that people have shoes. But I thought you meant to raise a political issue.

THOMAS NAGEL: I want to pose a further question. It seems to me that there are some cases of value conflict —for example over the allocation of public resources as between scientific research and social justice—where it would be absurd to say we should look for a redefinition of the value of scientific research so that it is restricted to the research that can be carried out with the money that would be available in a just allocation.

MR. DWORKIN: Right. That would be absurd.

MR. NAGEL: Why do you think that liberty and justice, or liberty and equality, are different—in the sense that when you arrive at a solution that you think is right you're going to want to translate it into a redefinition of the values so that the conflict between them disappears?

MR. DWORKIN: We've got a pretty good idea about what scientific research is and why it is important. We see that clearly enough to be confident that neither the correct understanding of what research is or the correct account of its value can depend on what rights people have, or any other distinctly political value. We may well improve our understanding of the character and point of science, but not by seeing these as interdependent with political ideals. But we are in a very different situation about liberty. First, we don't share anywhere near as clear an understanding of liberty as we do of research. It isn't as if, say, the negative liberty account that Mill and Berlin defend is satisfactory and we should just take it as it is. Bernard Williams said that that account leads to absurd conclusions, and I agree with that.

MR. WILLIAMS: Well, liberty as a political value.

MR. DWORKIN: Yes. So Thomas Nagel's question is: why do I think that the correct account of liberty, unlike research, might depend on other political values. I think so for two reasons: first, because we don't already have a settled conception of liberty. Unlike research, the true character of liberty is contested among us. And, second, because it's contested in a way that suggests rather than excludes its dependence on other values. We can see at once that what is the best method for discovering scientific truth does not in any way depend on what is the cheapest method. But it is far from clear that the best characterization of liberty does not make the boundaries of one person's liberty depend on the rights of others. On the contrary, for reasons I tried to suggest, that seems initially plausible.

In that case, you might ask, why should we argue about how liberty is best defined, particularly since we are unlikely to agree about that anyway? It's quite tempting to say: let's forget about liberty, and just try to decide what it's right and wrong for government to do without appealing to that idea. Or let's just stipulate some definition of liberty without any assumption that liberty is good and violating liberty is bad, leaving it open whether any particular compromise of liberty, defined in that way, is a good or bad thing. But we can't do that without impoverishing our political discourse. The people I mentioned, who say that when taxes go up liberty goes down, claim an analogy between putting someone in jail unjustly and taking his money in taxes. They're not just saying, in a general sort of way, that government ought to stop taxing people. They're not just offering a description of taxation and leaving it open whether taxation is good or bad. If we take the idea of liberty out of play, or make it only a descriptive notion, then we're denying them a point they think it important to make.

MR. WILLIAMS: Suppose we agree absolutely that liberty and justice aren't just given to you, that they need interpretation; let us agree that they have to be constructed. Why should we assume that it is an overwhelming aim of such interpretation or construction that it should remove the conflicts between them?

MR. DWORKIN: Well, of course I wouldn't put it that way: I wouldn't say that I aim to hide or submerge a conflict that is already there. The question is rather why I think we should aim to construct conceptions of our values—if we can find plausible such conceptions—that do not produce deep conflicts of the kind that we've been discussing. The answer seems to me obvious. If we accept a conflict we're accepting that whatever we do we're doing something wrong to people. And I would like, if possible, to construct a scheme of values that strike us as right but that do not entail that unpleasant conclusion. That seems to me a perfectly innocent aim. Of course, if we excavated or discovered conceptions of our values, that would be a silly aim. We could only aim to discover whatever was, as it were, the true DNA of liberty, equality, and the rest, and take our chances whether those DNA's conflicted. But, as you say, we don't find the right conceptions of our values in nature: we construct them, and integrity seems a reasonable aim, at least among others, of that process of construction.

NEIL RUDENSTINE: [President, Harvard University]: I wonder if the panel could comment on the extent to which Isaiah Berlin addresses the institutional context of conflict resolution. If there are ways to mitigate the sorts of conflicts we've been talking about, they are most likely to come within a context of institutional arrangements such that people feel that if they lose— and they really have lost—and they've lost something of value—nonetheless their judgment of the system as a whole leads them to say, "It's terrible; I've lost. But on balance I'd rather be here than there."

So I agree with Charles Taylor that every day, on every issue, in every conflict, you have to be an optimist and hope that you can find a resolution. At the same time, I feel it's a bit like the hydra—at least one head if not two will grow back every time you lop one off. From that point of view I'm more pessimistic. But if there is a long-range enterprise along the lines Thomas Nagel was describing, then I think an institutional arrangement is required, so that people can agree to the overarching principles and structures and still agree to lose.

MR. NAGEL: I think that that is where the solution lies. I actually can't say what Berlin's view was about this. As Steven Lukes said yesterday, he liked and believed in institutions. And certainly others who have been influenced by his pluralism, such as John Rawls, have taken it as support in particular for the kinds of liberal democratic institutions that will allow people who lose in such a contest to say, "I lost, and I genuinely lost something of value, but this is an acceptable outcome."

FRANCES KAMM: [Department of Philosophy, New York University]: I have a question for Ronald Dworkin. If someone is proposing theories of what is rightfully mine to do with what I want, and one of them would result in my being able to do practically nothing, presumably I would reject such a theory. It couldn't possibly be the right one, I would say, because it deprives me of too much liberty. Now, if I could raise that as an objection, isn't there some independent and prior sense of liberty by which I might select which theory is correctly telling me what is rightfully mine?

Second, I would like to ask if there is a relation between pluralism of values in Berlin and conflict of duties in Ross. There seem to be essential similarities. Ross also thought that there might be real incompatibilities at some level in our obligations, and not just because we'd gotten ourselves in a muddle by promising too many people things. For example, there might be real incompatibility between the duty to do justice and the duty to be merciful. This would be a case where one duty actually condemns the other. Was Berlin intellectually indebted to Ross for this concept?

MR. WILLIAMS: Well, I can answer the second part of the question. I think the answer to that is, "no." Berlin regarded Ross as roughly a sort of Aristotelian, rather too respectable. And I believe he thought that Ross's notion of the conflict of duties was insufficiently conflictual. Ross held that really there could only be a conflict between "*prima facie*" duties. Now, it is true that there was an ambiguity in Ross, because "*prima facie*" duty did not mean simply something that looked as though it might be a duty, but was not one. If a "*prima facie*" duty is not performed, there can be a negative residue. Berlin thought that the bit about the negative residue was indeed an acknowledgment of something which he would regard as ethically decent, but that Ross's ideas did not bring out the kind of conflict between real conceptions of what is worthwhile, which he felt to be the essence of what he himself was saying.

MR. DWORKIN: As for liberty and equality, if these values really are interconnected, as I think they are, then it would be no surprise that you could be frightened when you saw a bad account of equality because it seemed to leave you so little liberty. But it would work the other way as well: the scheme Frances Kamm describes strikes me as inegalitarian as well as illiberal because it would presumably work more against the interests of some people than others. I agree with you that we need what we might call prior convictions or intuitions or assumptions about both liberty and equality to think of the two as interconnected. We couldn't get very far defending a conception of liberty, on the ground that it was egalitarian, if it declared that locking people up when they weren't guilty wasn't a violation of their liberty.

If we accept the ambition of integrity I described, then we have to think in terms of solving simultaneous equations. We have to try and see our political values in the light of each other. But we must also respect the convictions that we begin with about the values themselves. So I agree with you, but I don't see the difficulty that you do.

MR. WOLLHEIM: I have an observation related to Mark Lilla's question, which I think was insufficiently taken up by the panel. It seems to me the panel has followed Ronald Dworkin's lead and has concentrated on conflicts that are (one) between persons, and so are interpersonal conflicts, and (two) are concerned largely with civic values, like justice. This has led to an interesting discussion, but is misleading as to Isaiah's views. For at least as interesting to Isaiah were *intra*personal conflicts, which seldom involve the civic virtues. They are more likely to involve things, for instance, like artistic creativity versus the comforts of life, or the call of patriotism versus cosmopolitanism. These were, I think, enormously important for Isaiah both as a theorist and in his own life. He thought quite rightly that they had been ignored in a rather more solemn form of philosophy.

Now, I think that if you take seriously this other kind of conflict, the kind of gerrymandering with values that Ronald Dworkin advocates is far less plausible. You can't shift your own private values in this way in order to produce peace, or inner harmony. Nor do I think that Berlin would have thought that this idea of concord within one's self at any cost, this idea, once again, of feeling at home, this somewhat nursery view of life, was all that attractive. I think he thought that leading one's life really was to expose one's self—not to extravagant Nietzschean-like conflicts—but to those different, irreducible pulls that made up the strangeness, and also the real authenticity, of life.

MR. DWORKIN: I certainly didn't mean to claim that our lives were always free from dramatic, even tragic, conflicts in personal values. Indeed, I tried to give examples of them. "Gerrymandering," as you put it, cannot relieve the tension of competing ideals from human lives. I said later, in answer to Mark Lilla, that we can often restate these conflicts as political issues, but that they look different, and may no longer present conflicts, when we do. But that depends on our political philosophy. If the perfect life would include achievements and experiences that simply can't all be realized in a single life, and if the job of government were to create the conditions in which people might lead perfect lives, then the personal conflict would indeed translate into a political one. But if we deny that government has any such responsibility, as I do, then this translation fails.

I want to respond to your use of "gerrymandering," however, because that suggests, as several other comments have, that I am twisting the meaning of a perfectly natural and clear concept—liberty—just to achieve a desirable political goal. But that is what I deny. The alternative to gerrymandering electoral districts is to accept compact, naturally shaped districts. But we have no such "natural" alternative in political philosophy. Certainly not in the case of liberty, because the only conception of that virtue that has gained currency even among political philosophers—the conception Isaiah Berlin endorsed—doesn't even seem eligible as a successful interpretation.

STEVEN LUKES: Now, I just wanted to put a rather specific question to Ronald Dworkin. I've noticed, by the way, that all the speakers have said they were optimistic. Whether they were optimistic about the same thing I'm not sure. But that of course is a great tribute to the Enlightenment.

Ronald Dworkin's optimism is that one can shape conceptions of liberal values so that they all hang together in the right way. And Bernard Williams in discussing this asked whether there was any reason for thinking it was so—or whether one would have to sacrifice some to others.

Now Ronald Dworkin actually did give an example of sacrifice, and I draw your attention to the fact that sacrifice is a religious metaphor—unlike trade-off, which is a commercial metaphor. Unlike sacrifices, I suggest, trade-offs can yield mutually acceptable compromises. And the example that he gave where the sacrifice was both intelligible and somehow understandable was Abraham and Isaac. So my question is, why is that example of Abraham and Isaac somehow set apart and not related to the rest of the discussion? Why is that somehow special?

MR. DWORKIN: I cited Abraham and Isaac—as an example of a case in which someone might reasonably be certain that his values were in conflict—mainly to show why the case of liberty and equality is very different. If we imagine, as might well have seemed plausible in the ancient world, that God and parental duty are two independent sovereigns, so that we can understand the commands of each without attending to the commands of the other, and if we understand that God has commanded a sacrifice that personal duty forbids, then we are not merely uncertain whether the commands can be reconciled, but certain that they cannot be. Of course, not all religious people would accept that premise about the independence of God and personal morality: some would say that we cannot understand God unless we see him as moral, and others that we cannot understand morality except as the word of God. My example depended on theological independence rather than interdependence.

But we cannot see from the start that liberty and equality must conflict because we do not start with a clear and persuasive account of liberty that shows liberty to be independent of other values in the way that God's command might be thought to be independent of any personal morality. On the contrary, we start with these facts: that the character of liberty is contested among us, that we are obliged to develop interpretations or conceptions of that ideal, and that conceptions that show liberty to be independent of other values, like Berlin's definition of negative liberty, seem defective for that reason. We might well find, in the end, after we have done our best, keeping faith, as Frances Kamm reminds us that we must, with our recalcitrant intuitions, that the best conceptions of liberty, equality, and democracy do make each of these values independent of the others. It might turn out that the cases we have been discussing are much more like the case of Abraham and Isaac than I suppose. But we must do all that work. We cannot simply declare, as Abraham might have declared, for conflict right away.

Part III

NATIONALISM AND ISRAEL

ROBERT SILVERS

Introduction

IN THINKING ABOUT our subject this afternoon—nationalism and Zionism—I came across a printed exchange
between Isaiah Berlin and the Iranian philosopher and
journalist Ramin Jahanbegloo. Mr. Jahanbegloo asked
Isaiah Berlin whether he would consider Chaim Weizmann a Romantic figure, and Isaiah replied as follows:

> Anybody who could conceive and create a new
> people out of scattered members of a religious
> community or race after more than two thousand
> years must have a Romantic imagination. It's cer-
> tainly a challenge to realism, and yet Weizmann,
> so far as I know, was deeply realistic. But he under-
> stood something very real about the Jews, namely
> that few human beings in the end want to remain
> members of a minority in every society. He under-
> stood instinctively that people can only develop
> freely (as Herder thought, of whom Weizmann,
> so far as I can tell, had never heard) in a country
> in which they are not perpetually uneasy about
> what other people think about them, how they

look to others, does their behavior attract unfa-
vorable or perhaps too much attention—are they
accepted. Is it all right?

I quote this statement because it seems to contain
within it many of the themes we are here to discuss this
afternoon: the project of a Jewish national home, which
Isaiah Berlin supported all his life, and how it fits with
the other principles of his thought.

That he cited Herder in replying to the Iranian
philosopher about Weizmann recalls, of course, one of
the central projects of his work—his tracing, both in
thought and in actual history, of the revolt against the
principles of the Enlightenment on which the French
Revolution was founded. The principles, that is, of a
peaceful universalism and rational humanitarianism,
and the idea, as he put it, of a "single, scientifically
organized world system." Much of Isaiah Berlin's work
was devoted to showing how such principles came to be
challenged—challenged, he wrote in his essay on Herder,
by the craving for fraternity and self-expression that
dominated so much of the nineteenth century, and even
more our own, as one form of nationalism or another
asserted itself. The process by which this happened, he
said, was often mysterious, but, he wrote, "it would
not be an exaggeration to say that no political movement today, at least in the West, seems likely to succeed
unless it allies itself with nationalism." And in the
political movement of Zionism he found a nationalism
he could support. And then we note that when Isaiah
Berlin talked about Weizmann's dream, it was of a

people "developing freely," and we know that, for him, developing freely, in whatever national setting, meant not simply the freedom to realize one's national destiny but protection of the most important liberties from interference by the state. And so the question arose, and was much on his mind, of the liberty not only of Jews but of Palestinians to develop freely both within the Jewish state and outside it, in a state of their own. These are among the questions that face us this afternoon.

AVISHAI MARGALIT

The Crooked Timber of Nationalism

ISAIAH BERLIN HAD a keen interest in famous last words. The last words of Chaim Weizmann, as they were reported to Berlin by Weizmann's doctor, amused and troubled him. Amused him for their wit and presence of mind, troubled him for their expression of intense bitterness. On his deathbed, Weizmann coughed terribly, and felt that he was choking. His doctor told him to spit. "There's no one left worth spitting at," gasped Weizmann, in Yiddish, and died.

Weizmann was for Berlin the epitome of a non-neurotic Jew. Yet, in the days that the state of Israel was established, he felt lonely and bitter. A friend who visited him at his home asked him what he was doing these days, to which Weizmann replied, "Doing? They tell me that as a president of Israel I symbolize the country, so I sit the whole day and symbolize." Weizmann in his home struck Berlin as a homeless King Lear. But then, the whole point of Zionism was to provide the Jews with a sense of home.

When Ben-Gurion, the dialectical rival of Weizmann, and the one most responsible for Weizmann's bitterness, asked Isaiah Berlin to become the head of the foreign office, and later asked Albert Einstein to succeed Weizmann as president of Israel, they both turned him down. They both recognized the need for home, and the need for a national home for the Jews, but both believed that immigrating to Israel is a matter of personal choice, and both rejected integralist Zionism which made it a matter of fate as well as a test of Jewish authenticity.

Berlin was not like those people who became Zionists because they couldn't stand being Jews. He was utterly secure as a Jew and as a Zionist. He was very attentive to the needs of ordinary people, without a trace of the elitist bias of intellectuals who tend to project their privileged needs on ordinary people and to disregard the needs of common people which do not match their own. Berlin did not personally need a home in Israel, but he believed that many Jews did.

Classical Zionism viewed Zionism as the solution to anti-Semitism. Not so Isaiah Berlin. In his mind, the emphasis was not on anti-Semitism as such, but rather on one of its effects, namely, the Jewish loss of a sense of home. Berlin stuck to the definition of anti-Semitism as hating the Jews beyond necessity. At the same time, he knew better than others the refined forms that anti-Semitism can take, by people who hate Jews and also hate anti-Semites because, among other things, they find both types too vulgar. Classical Zionism had in mind a virulent form of anti-Semitism. Berlin knew that even subdued forms of anti-Semitism are effective enough in making Jews not feel at ease, in depriving them of spontaneity and natural forms of behavior, in causing them to become over-self-conscious. For good reasons the Jew became a metaphor for the existential plight of the so-called modern man, but his plight was more concrete and less metaphysical. Berlin once asked me, "What do you think is common to all the Jews? I mean, to the Jew from Sana and from Marakesh, from Riga and from Golders Green?" And right away he himself answered, "A sense of social unease. Nowhere do Jews feel entirely at home."

Berlin, like his mentor Weizmann, was an instinctive Zionist, not an ideological one. He did not feel the need to justify his Zionism. Zionism obviously calls for a great deal of justification, since, no matter how you slice it, for the Jews to regain a home meant for Palestinian Arabs to lose theirs. This troubled Berlin, but not to the point of seriously questioning his Zionism. He viewed Zionism as an immanent move in Jewish history. Once the Orthodox ghetto ceases to be an option of life, and assimilation is not an option of life either, Zionism is the natural solution. At the same time, Berlin never considered Zionism as plain common sense. He relished quoting Weizmann as saying, "You don't have to be crazy in order to be a Zionist, but it helps." The "crazy" element in Zionism was the odds against its success. To believe that a scattered nation will be able, just fifty years after the first Zionist congress, to establish a state in the land of Israel with 650,000 of its people, and that fifty years later it will be home to five million Jews, called for a great leap of faith.

Berlin was not a Zionist fellow-traveler who believed

that in Israel a utopia was being materialized except that it was not understood by a hostile outside world. He was not an apologetic defender of a utopia, because he had very few illusions about the Jews and about the nature of the state of Israel. The illusion that the state of Israel was a light unto the nations was not one of them. He viewed Israel as a sensible solution to a concrete plight of the Jews. My claim is, or to put it more pompously, my thesis is, that Berlin's Zionism was not an ideology which derives from primary principles such as nationalism or liberalism. His Zionism was for him more akin to a family business than to a doctrine. Yet Berlin's version of Zionism tallies with the emotions that underlie his version of nationalism.

For Berlin the emotional underpinnings of nationalism are the most important element in nationalism, more important than the set of beliefs that nourishes it. Altogether, Berlin's interest was in the emotions, feelings, and moods which motivate social movements, even more than in their ideas. His concern was not the pure philosophical concern with sense, but with sensibility, a concern with the systematic ties between ideas and feelings. Like Hume, he believed that what motivates people are feelings and emotions—not reason. Though feelings without ideas are blind, ideas without feelings are dead, and he was interested in what is alive. The last point is important for understanding Berlin's intellectual undertaking.

Isaiah Berlin was what Nietzsche called *Psychologue*, and what the French called *moraliste*, which is neither a psychologist nor a moralist in the current use of these terms. A *Psychologue* is a person, usually a writer and especially a novelist, who has the capacity, through empathy, to put himself into the working of the human soul, cutting through appearances and words. A *moraliste* in the French sense is not someone who is morally high minded. His concern is not moral judgment, but to see through layers of conventions, customs, and social appearances what really makes people tick. Thus Berlin is a *Psychologue* and a *moraliste*. Though he was a great believer in the morality of liberalism, he never trusted its psychology, especially not that which derived from the psychology of the Enlightenment, which he found downright silly. When it came to the psychology of nationalism, it was Romanticism to which he turned for insight.

What, according to Berlin, are the emotions which motivate nationalism? Wanting to belong is a strong motivation: be it to a family, a clan, a tribe, or, in our time, to a nation. You want to belong not in virtue of what you do—but to belong in virtue of what you are. You want your belonging not to be conditional on your achievements. You can't fail, say, in being Irish. Modern life, stressing as it does competition and achievement, created the emotional antidote to belonging. Modern life eroded the family, the clan, and the tribe to the point where the nation became the main substitute for primary belonging.

Belonging ties in Berlin's thought with the sense of home. Berlin, in fact, adopts Robert Frost's definition, "Home is the place where, when you go there, they have to take you in. I should have called it something you somehow haven't to deserve." This notion of *home* as a place that cannot turn you down if you belong, is at the foundation of what I take to be the problematic but the constitutive law of Israel as a Zionist state, namely the law of return, which decrees that every Jew in the world is entitled to unconditional Israeli citizenship.

What is so great about feeling at home? Isaiah Berlin sees an intimate connection between feeling at home and being free. When a guest of ours asks "may I use this or that," we sometimes answer "feel free," or "feel at home"—the two are interchangeable. This domestic observation captures that which is for Berlin a deep connection between feeling at home and being free, namely the ability to behave naturally and spontaneously. This, for Berlin, is great. Now in addition to the two emotions that propel nationalism already mentioned, i.e., a sense of belonging and a sense of home, Berlin mentions a third one: humiliation, in the sense of national humiliation. This was the most pronounced emotion in the shaping of German nationalism. It is encapsulated in the metaphor of the "bent twig." "Bent" alludes to the humiliating conquest of the nation by a foreign power which is recognized as more advanced and culturally more sophisticated. But then, since it is a bent *twig*, the twig eventually turns into a whip, to lash at the nation's tormenters.

Of these three emotions—craving for belonging, yearning for home, and feeling humiliated—which played a role in shaping Zionism? The lack of the sense of belonging and home definitely played a crucial role in Zionism. This role, however, was different from that played with regard to a normal nation whose people have lived in territorial proximity for generations. Belonging to the Jewish people does not mean belonging to a nation whose people are like you. Because Jews were dispersed for so many generations, they were very unlike each other. So in the Jewish case, to belong to your kin does not mean to belong to your ilk. As to the sense of home, if being at home means being *in* a home (that is, in a shared territory), the Jews lacked territory. But Berlin believed that belonging to the Jewish community in the land of Israel will form the conditions for creating, or restoring, a sense of home among Jews. He believed that for the Jews who immigrated to Israel, Israel succeeded in creating a sense of home. It is said that when Hermann Cohen, the great Neo-Kantian philosopher, was told about Zionism, he reacted with derision: "So these guys want to be happy?" Franz Rosenzweig and Gershom Scholem were both troubled by this reaction of Cohen's. It made them worry that maybe the aim of Zionism is not lofty enough. Berlin would have reacted differently. Jews on his account don't even ask to be happy—which for him is a great thing in itself—they just want to feel at home.

As to the third emotion, that of national humiliation, it is clear that Jews were badly humiliated throughout their history, both as individuals and as a group. But the grassroots of the Zionist movement in Eastern Europe did not feel national humiliation in its modern manifestation, which is being conquered by a nation whose culture is considered superior to and more advanced than their own. It is true that some Zionist leaders in Western Europe did feel that way, and Herzl, the founder of modern Zionism, was indeed motivated by an acute sense of national humiliation. But Herzl had very little understanding of the Zionism of yearning for a sense of home. Herzl's willingness to accept Uganda as a solution for the Jews shows how differently motivated he was from his people. Herzl the leader was in this respect educated by his followers.

So far I've talked about Isaiah Berlin's ideas of the emotions that underlie modern nationalism. But what is modern nationalism? According to Berlin it is the conviction that human beings belong to particular human groups, and that the form of life of each group differs from all the others. It is the conviction that the characters of the individuals in the group are shaped by the group and can be understood only with reference to the group's customs, language, religion, shared memories and social institutions. In some racist form of nationalism, heredity and racial traits are added. This set of beliefs is different from the old national sentiment based on tribal feelings and pride of ancestry. It is a modern doctrine. To this doctrine Berlin adds another feature, viewing the nation, or its form of life, as an organism.

The metaphor of the nation as an organism has many and varied uses. One use stresses the unity within the apparent multiplicity in the national existence, another stresses the purposefulness of the nation, still another the orderly division among its sub-groups (or "organs") which are mutually dependent. But the most dangerous, illiberal use of the organism metaphor, at least for Berlin, is that which accords moral precedence to the whole (the nation) over its individuals. On this view the nation is the tree, and the individuals are mere leaves. The precedence takes the form of making the goal of the nation an overriding reason for the individual. Berlin, who believed that nationalistic movements are guided more by feelings and the imagination than by reason and doctrine, took their metaphors more seriously than he took their claims. He knew that the troubling metaphor of the integralist Zionists is neither the tree and the leaves, nor the bent twig, but instead it is the metaphor of the roots.

The traditional Right describes Zionism as the project of striking roots, both in the holy geography of the land of Israel, from which the nation was uprooted and which are mostly located in the West Bank territories, and in the hearts, i.e., spiritual roots which will turn the nation into a religious or at least a traditionalist community. There is much irony in the fact that the accusation leveled at the Jews by their detractors, of being rootless cosmopolitans, is now being turned in Israel against the Left. Isaiah Berlin did not like the root metaphor. He thought that human beings are endowed with brains and hearts, not with roots. He was afraid that the integralists lost their brains and hardened their hearts in their endeavor to strike roots.

Yet, perhaps because he was the son of a timber merchant, Berlin himself was attracted to tree metaphors. He made the bent-twig metaphor known, and he made Kant's crooked-timber metaphor famous. "Out of timber so crooked," writes Kant, "as that from which man is made, nothing entirely straight can be carved." Berlin, I believe, knew well that the gloss on Kant's "crooked-timber" metaphor is complicated. In the article in which Kant writes about the crooked timber of humanity ("Idea for a Universal History with a Cosmopolitan Purpose") he invokes another metaphor. He compares man living in isolation to man living in a proper civil society. "Trees in the forest, by seeking to deprive each other of air and sunlight, compel each other to find these by upward growth, so that they grow beautiful and straight—whereas those who put out branches at will, in freedom and isolation from others, grow stunted, bent and twisted." I believe that Kant contrasts natural trees to timber. And he contrasts between natural growth in society, which is like a tree in the wood, and a designed artifact made of timber, which is like the shaping of society according to an artificial plan. The crooked timber, then, is a metaphor against the shaping of human society according to a blueprint.

Isaiah Berlin was vehemently against *a priori* planning for a whole society. But then the question, forcefully raised by Stuart Hampshire, arises, how to reconcile Berlin's objection to *a priori* blueprints with Zionism given that Zionism was a blueprint ideology, imposed on the crooked timber of the Jews with the hope of straightening them up. I believe that there is genuine tension between Berlin's objection to wholesale blueprint ideologies on the one hand, and his adoption of Zionism on the other. But then I maintain that Berlin's

Zionism belonged to his "base," not to his "super-structure," whereas liberalism and cultural nationalism belonged to his "superstructure." It is not easy to doctrinally reconcile Berlin's Zionism with all the "isms" that belonged to his superstructure: they simply belong to different layers in his soul.

It is an irony of fate that Isaiah Berlin, so many of whose utterances were memorable and quotable, didn't himself utter famous last words. But the ones that he did are pertinent to our topic. At the end of October 1997 I received from Isaiah a letter that surprised me. It contained a statement, the title of which is "Israel and the Palestinians." It reads as follows:

> Since both sides begin with a claim of total possession of Palestine as their historical right, and since neither claim can be accepted within the realm of realism or without grave injustice, it is plain that compromise, i.e. partition, is the only correct solution, along Oslo lines—for supporting which Rabin was assassinated by a Jewish bigot.
>
> Ideally, what we are calling for is a relationship of good neighbors, but given the number of bigoted, terrorist chauvinists on both sides, this is impracticable.
>
> The solution must lie somewhat along the lines of reluctant toleration, for fear of far worse—i.e., a savage war which could inflict irreparable damage on both sides.
>
> As for Jerusalem, it must remain the capital of Israel, with the Muslims' holy places being

extraterritorial to a Muslim authority, with a guarantee from the United Nations of preserving that position, by force if necessary.

To this statement, Berlin added a personal note, on a separate sheet of paper:

This is my formula: of any use to anyone? If not— waste paper basket.

I thought the note meant that the statement should be published in the Israeli press, but I wanted his explicit permission. Lady Berlin asked for his permission just before he was taken in for the operation from which he didn't recover. The fax from Lady Berlin, dated November fifth, read: "Isaiah says 'yes.'" For all I can tell, this was perhaps his last word.

What was so surprising was not the content of the letter, but the very fact that he wrote it. All his life Berlin was wary of expressive politics. He believed that political action should be carried out only when there was a reasonable chance that it would make a difference. Being expressive was, for him, the realm of art; being effective, the realm of politics. What counts in politics is only that which changes the course of events. But here was something different: in his last statement he simply wanted to stand up and be counted.

In his discussion of nationalism Berlin was struck by the fact that the prophets of the nineteenth century were right on target in predicting some important features of our century. But they were blind to one major feature: the role of nationalism. They believed it would play no role. When it comes to Zionism, there were two prophecies pointing in opposite directions. One was that of Lillienblum and several other leading Zionists, who predicted that the state of the Jews will become a Switzerland in the Middle East, with Jews and Arabs living in separate cantons. The other prophecy was that of the old fox Tolstoy, according to which Zionism will end up as Serbia of the Middle East, aggressive and expansionist. Isaiah Berlin hoped for a Switzerland and feared a Serbia, and expected that it would be something in between. He was hopeful after the Oslo agreement, but in the last year of his life he feared that the old fox Tolstoy saw something big and terrifying and real. Hence the letter.

RICHARD WOLLHEIM

Berlin and Zionism

I FIND IT odd and very poignant to be talking this afternoon in a public space about a theme in Berlin's work
which the two of us, in a close friendship of over fifty
years never discussed, except glancingly. Since we had
contrasting views on this matter, some might think that
our agreement not to discuss the topic, solemnized for
me in a dream I had, which I then recounted to Isaiah
the next day, was an attempt to safeguard our friendship. I, for reasons that may emerge by the end of this
talk, prefer to think that our agreement was a sign, a
manifestation, of our friendship. Not a varnish that
was placed over it to protect it.

Let me begin by distinguishing two belief systems.
One belief system is constituted by the belief in national
self-determination. According to this system, every
nation on the face of this earth is entitled to its own
homeland: this homeland being an expanse of soil to
which it has strong historical connections, unsevered
over a period of time, where it may live according to its
own culture and practice its own religion and its own
secular habits. There it may speak its own language or

languages, enjoy peace, and presumably prepare for war. This entitlement is, according to the belief in national self-determination, constrained to some degree by the nation's willingness to respect, again, to some degree, similar entitlements on the part of those nations with whom it is required to share its homeland.

The other belief system consists of the various discrete specific nationalisms, each identified by the nation whose claim to its own homeland it proclaims. Generally, nationalisms have their own preselected adherents, or those who belong, or think that they belong, to the nation in question. But there have also been those noble spirits like Byron or Roger Casement who transcended such parochialisms.

The adherent of a discrete nationalism may or may not believe in national self-determination as a principle. Zionism is a discrete nationalism, and one which Berlin supported, despite his hostility to the Jewish religion. Or perhaps I should say despite his hostility to religion, from which hostility to the Jewish religion might be inferred. Berlin further supported the state of Israel, though he strongly disapproved of some of the means by which it came about, and a number of the means by which it sought to preserve itself.

On a superficial view of the matter, Zionism might seem to be a rather problematic form of nationalism: compared say, to Kurdish nationalism or the American Indian movement. For Zionism is confronted with at least four serious difficulties.

The first is the problem of how the nation is defined, or who or what is a Jew. There are, we know, a number of ways of answering this question which are fully declarative, like say, the Nuremberg laws or, I take it, the law of return. But these are not consistent with one another. The only time that I have ever been asked this question about myself, which was put to me by a kindly-looking German general during the five days I was a prisoner of war, I think I used the ambiguity which I've just referred to, to give, I suppose, a conveniently evasive answer.

Berlin, as I understood it, had no single answer to the question, though he sometimes suggested that anyone who thought himself a Jew was one. What this answer does to the case for Zionism is another matter. And I never heard Berlin express the view that anyone who thought of himself as not a Jew was not one. On the contrary, Berlin concurred with Moses Hess in his denunciation of assimilation, which he seems to have equated with someone who was a Jew not thinking of himself as one. Then, of course, the question arises, "A Jew by what criterion?" An issue, which as far as I know Berlin never confronted, is the case of someone who is a Jew by some acceptable criterion and thinks of this as a relatively unimportant fact about himself or herself.

Secondly, on any plausible resolution of the first question, "Who is a Jew?," it seems likely that the Jewish nation, defined according to it, will turn out to be far from culturally homogenous. Hence it becomes to some degree uncertain what life in the homeland will foster. This is, I take it, something brought out by the current demography of Israel.

Thirdly, at least before 1947, the connection

between the Jewish nation and the favored geographical homeland, or Palestine, is not historically dense. Rather, it is mediated by a deep institutionalized memory and by the various rituals of a religion from which Zionism has often tried to disassociate itself. Fourthly, from the early days of Zionism there seemed to be built-in reasons why the entitlements of the Jewish nation to its homeland might very well clash with claims of other indigenous peoples. Berlin's powerful portrait of Weizmann, which despite its measured praise is at any rate to my ears, but I don't think to everyone's ears, colored by ambivalence, feeds these doubts.

I've said that to think of these four points as constituting anything of a case against Zionism is to take a superficial view of the matter. And what I had in mind was it failed to take account of how discrete nationalisms are justified. It rides roughshod over the question how the belief in national self-determination is grounded. It is, I think, for illumination on these matters, that I turn to the writings of Berlin.

On this score I have heard it said that for Berlin the justification of nationalism was just part and parcel of the general lesson about mankind that nineteenth-century Romanticism had to teach eighteenth-century rationalism. That man has fundamental needs beyond those which arise out of the exigencies of life, and these include the need for a community in which he can discover his identity. This is what nationalism provides. Hence its justification. Now, though there is some plausibility in this reconstruction of Berlin's thinking, I believe that it ignores the crucial fact that for him, as so often, Romanticism constructed what on this view it is supposed to have discovered. Nationalism, Berlin says on many occasions, is a construct of Romanticism. And so, for much of the time in his thinking, is that sense of identity that nationalism is supposed to generate.

It is, I think, significant as far as this last point is concerned that the most sustained investigation we have of the sense of identity in the context of Jewishness that is to be found in Berlin's writings is apropos of Disraeli and Marx. Both, according to Berlin, were ill at ease with their Jewishness, so that one denied it and the other aggrandized it out of existence. And both thereby found a working form of life. However, it is worth pointing out that in Berlin's discussion both of Disraeli and of Marx the sense of identity that is considered there is a radically de-psychologized version of the phenomenon, compared for instance to that which figures in what we might think of as regular communitarianism, in which there is a very psychologized version of this quest for identity.

The clearest reference I know to another conception of the sense of identity occurs, again, in Berlin's *éloge* of Weizmann where we find a memorable and, to my ear, daunting phrase, "He lived the full life of a Jew." I have to say I do not understand what this means, any more than I would have understood the phrase, "He lived the full life of an Englishman."

So we are thrown back, I think, on more conventional justifications of nationalism and thus derivatively, Zionism. And the question now arises, where does Berlin stand as far as these more standard justifications are concerned? We may think of such justifications as divided into the positive and the negative.

Positive justifications stress what the nation will be able to offer the world from a secure homeland. Negative justifications stress how a secure homeland would shelter the nation from the world.

It was not in Berlin's nature to produce positive justifications for Zionism. He was, I suspect, far too sensitive to the distorting effects of subjectivity to make claims on behalf of the Jewish contribution to civilization. Even Freud, who deplored the departure from Mediterranean sunniness that he found in Judaism, thought that the ethical legacy of the Jewish tradition was an inestimable boon to the world. As far as I can see, Berlin thought it better and more in keeping, I think, with his own temperament, to refrain from such claims, and his often repeated sentiment that if there were a pill that Jews could take that would turn them overnight into Danes, he would favor their taking it, is not only compatible with Berlin's modesty on the issue of a positive justification for Zionism, but steers us, I believe, in the direction of the negative justification for Zionism that he favored.

For Berlin, as I see it, Zionism was ultimately justified by the existence of anti-Semitism. Without a doubt, anti-Semitism provides a justification for Zionism. How profound a justification or how appropriate a response Zionism is to anti-Semitism depends, I believe, ultimately on the view that we take of what anti-Semitism is. More precisely, it depends on this: how seriously embedded is the concept of Jewishness in anti-Semitism? Or does it figure there simply as a pretext for what would otherwise be free-floating aggression? Is anti-Semitism grounded in hostility to characteristics that Jews—all Jews, that is, actually possess?

If you think that the answer to this question is yes, then you are likely to think two things. First, that the case for a national homeland is very strong, though you might also think that where it proves possible to establish such a homeland the need for it is likely to be at least in abeyance. Secondly, you might think this: that, though it might be prudent for Jews to conceal the characteristics that provoke anti-Semitism, it would not be the course either of pride or of dignity to do so.

If however, you believe that anti-Semitism is only associatively connected with what Jews are actually like, then though the preceding course of action is still open to you, there are other courses that are also open. One might, for instance, be inclined to think that what Zionism does is that it lends an artificial weight or homogeneity to the very concept of the Jew, and hence it tends to reinforce the prejudices that it is trying to confront.

I can quote only from my own experience. When in the mid-1930s I was thirteen or fourteen, and members of my father's family began to arrive in England, chased out as Jews, though I also knew that other members of the same family were allowed to stay there as Aryans, I tried to find out why this was so, and what it was that was so distinctive about being a Jew. The answer that I was given to this question was that to think of someone—and this is presumably including one's self—as a Jew, was the first step on the way to anti-Semitism. I have to say that, religious issues and issues of deep cultural conditioning apart, I still believe that something like this is true. Berlin did not. And I tend to think that the forces that drove us in different directions on this very issue are so deep and can be excavated only with such intense difficulty that it was quite right to think that discussion of these differences should not come up between friends.

I conclude on an aspect of Berlin's Zionism that I believe fitted in awkwardly with his general attitude to life, with what he gave to life and what he hoped to derive from it. Broadly speaking, people may be divided into those who like communities, those who like institutions, and those who regard both as necessary interferences, but interferences all the same, with personal life. Berlin, as I thought of him, liked institutions, not communities. In this regard, he made really something of an exception in favor of Zionism. In consequence, when he reverted to the attitude which I think of as coming more naturally to him, he did show himself less than sympathetic to other nationalisms with their communitarian bases. And this may have had the effect, I think, of obscuring the extraordinary generosity of sentiment that he brought to topics that have generally aroused all the sentiments and attitudes that he, Isaiah, most disliked.

MICHAEL WALZER

Liberalism, Nationalism, Reform

IMAGINE SOMEBODY WHO has strong attachments to a particular group of people—I mean, a group in the strong sense of the word, not a temporary grouping, not an interest group, not an association for this or that purpose, but an anciently established ethnic or national community or a "community of faith" (that's the current term, though the community of faith to which I belong, at least in my experience of it, consists mostly of people without faith). He wants this particular group to survive and prosper, to find a secure place in the world, to live in peace. It's not that he doesn't want similar things for other groups, but the wanting, in the case of the others, is the product of a general good will, while the wanting, in the particular case, is, so to speak, personal; it's intense, sustained, brooded over. This is what he wants all the time and with feeling. Of course, he wants what is right in all cases, but he isn't even-handed in his wanting.

Now imagine also that the world in which all groups of this kind, all strong groups, coexist is a hard world. Wealth, land, prestige, and power are scarce within it.

So the coexistence is political in character, which is to say, competitive and conflictual; the interests of the groups are not harmonious or not necessarily or always harmonious. Sometimes the groups are only loosely at odds, competing in a routinized way for members or political influence or private or public funding; sometimes they are very tensely at odds; sometimes they are at war with one another.

So the question is: how does this person sustain his attachment and seek to achieve what he wants for his own group while still living a moral life and willing with a good will? I can think of three possible answers to this question—I know that they are "possible" answers because I have heard many people arguing in these ways (and I think that you have too).

1. He can pretend that the world isn't really hard, or isn't as hard as realists-about-the-world claim that it is, or isn't hard right now, in this particular case, in these circumstances. The interests that he so passionately defends are or can be made consistent with all the other interests to which he is, in general, committed.

2. He can argue that there is something special about the group to which he is attached, or something unique in its current situation or recent history, that justifies the precedence he gives to its interests. He wants what he wants for this group not only with his particular will but also with his general will. And, he argues, all good people who understand the specialness or the uniqueness, whatever their own attachments, will want the same thing.

3. He can try to universalize his own case—

acknowledging that other groups have legitimate interests to which their members are as passionately committed as he is to the interests of his group. The resulting conflicts may sometimes be open to judgments of just and unjust, but often they are not; and when they are not there are no settlements without moral and material losses to one group or another. He will seek as best he can, he says, to minimize the losses to his own group, but he insists at the same time that he respects similar efforts by people on the other side. All that a general good will can require in such cases, he says, is that neither side deliberately seek to injure, humiliate, or destroy the other, that each work toward a settlement that preserves the existing plurality of attachments and interests. The recognition of pluralism requires mutual accommodation, but this is an accommodation reached at the bargaining table, and it is morally acceptable, he says, to sit on one side of the table.

I think that this is, though short, an exhaustive list of the possibilities. The only alternatives to these three are to give up the particular attachments or to give up the general good will. It's probably fair to say that giving up the particular attachments is the preferred course of action among moral philosophers, perhaps among political theorists too (there are obviously dissenters in both groups), while giving up the general good will is the common course among political actors—though the actors or their intellectual supporters are likely to produce some ideological disguise for their surrender by making one or another of the three arguments I have just described. But the first two of these three lend themselves more readily than the last one to such ideological uses.

In fact, I am inclined to say that the first two are almost always ideological, in Marx's or Mannheim's precise sense, involving systematically distorted claims about the world. That means, first, that the conflicts in which such arguments are made can't, in fact, be resolved without losses—the realists are right; and second, that while every group is special if viewed from some particular perspective with reference to some particular issue, the specialness required to support the claims made on its behalf in the midst of a struggle with other groups—that kind of specialness just doesn't exist. So the argument from a harmony of interests and the argument from specialness don't work, and, much of the time (though not in every case), it's hard to believe that the people who make them don't know this—so that the arguments often seem to involve a kind of bad faith.

The third way of bringing together particular attachments with general good will, the appeal to pluralism, was Isaiah Berlin's way, and I think that it is the right way, indeed, the only way—though there is plenty of room for argument about what it involves in any given case, including, obviously, the Zionist case. What makes it necessary, again, is the refusal to give up the particular attachments or the general good will. A great deal of Isaiah Berlin's work can be understood as an effort to explore all the consequences—historical, political, and philosophical—of these two refusals. The political position that results from the two is some kind of liberal nationalism.

Liberal Nationalism is the title of a book by Yael Tamir that was originally a doctoral dissertation written with Isaiah Berlin, perhaps the last one, certainly one of the last, that he directed. I can't claim that Tamir's doctrine is Berlin's, but it is at least compatible with his two refusals. What it involves, it seems to me (I'm not going to try to repeat the argument of her book), is a modification of nationalism and a complication of liberalism. Nationalism is modified in two ways: first, its protagonists are required to recognize the collective rights of other nations (to self-determination, sovereignty, autonomy, or whatever); and second, they are required, and this may be harder, to recognize the rights of the members of their own nation as individual men and women (so the nation can't be conceived as an integral union with a single interest and a single will). Liberalism is complicated because it is required to engage with and adjust to an alien particularism, which it can only modify, which it can't (like any adjective that precedes a noun) wholly transform. Liberal nationalists are attached men and women who respect the attachments of the others—without pretending that "respect," in practice, is going to be easy. I want to insist that this acceptance of uneasiness isn't a question of principle. The Italian patriot and general issue militant, Giuseppe Mazzini, was a liberal nationalist, perhaps the first of the breed, who seems to have believed, without apparent unease, that he could support every nationalist movement in Europe; he wanted to dance at every wedding. It is a lesson of experience, not a deduction from a set of principles, that nationalism generates conflict and that the respect liberal nationalists owe to other nations doesn't preclude opposing (some of) their demands. Nor does attachment to one's own nation preclude opposing some of the demands of fellow nationals.

Liberal nationalists accept the principle of national self-determination—first of all in their own case and then for the nation that comes next. I think of "the nation that comes next" as the critical moral test. So Iraqi nationalists are tested by the Kurds, Algerian nationalists by the Berbers, and Zionists, of course, by the Palestinians. The tests don't always have the same character, and they don't always require the same resolution. Self-determination can take different political forms—full democracy and equal citizenship is a possible way of dealing with pluralism; various versions of decentralization and autonomy offer more room for communal self-government and cultural reproduction; separation, sovereignty, and statehood provide as much room as the modern world (and the global economy) allows. For the Palestinians today, statehood and sovereignty are morally required, as Isaiah Berlin recognized most clearly in his last political statement.

There is no better evidence of the possibility of my third option, of pluralism and liberal nationalism, than the actual existence of nationalists who are liberals. The fact that large numbers of nationalists are not liberals isn't counter-evidence; it merely defines the opposition that liberal nationalists encounter and have to deal with. Passionate and particularist attachments are obviously not always modified in a liberal way, but they can be modified; they sometimes have been. We can see this, perhaps with greater clarity, in the sphere of family relations, where liberal parents accept that their children should be subject to impartial procedures in, say, educational grading, or college admissions, or civil service examinations. They may seek some special help for their own children, but they will recognize the right of other parents to do the same thing, and they will acknowledge the need for some constraints on the exercise of this right (though they are likely to disagree on the extent of the constraints).

I don't think that the modification of collective attachments is necessarily any more difficult than this —though it commonly takes place, when it takes place, in a more difficult setting, one that fosters suspicion and distrust. Sometimes, nonetheless, collective attachments are easier to modify than personal attachments are, since the modification is, at least initially, notional, and the policies that it requires one to support are likely to have only longterm and impersonal effects. In any case, there are not only individuals, like Isaiah Berlin, who hold the modified position but also significant political factions, tendencies, and movements. Zionist history provides us with a useful and heartening example of modification—in the politics that led to the Oslo agreement and the politics that might have followed upon the agreement if Rabin had not been assassinated (and if he had been re-elected). What has actually followed is less heartening, but still suggests, at least, that liberal nationalism has some capacity for endurance.

Nonetheless, it is often said that nationalism can't (really) be modified; it has to be opposed always and everywhere because it is essentially extreme—just as one might say (though I don't believe that anyone actually says this) that parental love must be opposed because it is essentially extreme. This is exactly the position that Isaiah Berlin rejected, not only because he was, in general, an anti-essentialist but also because he was, in particular, a liberal Zionist. There is also, I think, a practical argument against any such essentialism: liberals who adopt it set themselves irrevocably against the passions of attachment. And that is an opposition in which they will never be successful. They aim at a kind of revolutionary transformation of everyday human life—at the creation of a "new liberal man (woman)," not so different from the "new socialist man" that was the ostensible goal of the Soviet educational system and for which the totalitarian politics on which that system rested is no doubt necessary (but not sufficient). And this sort of thing would seem to violate the "essence" of liberalism. . . .

Liberal nationalism is probably best understood as a species of liberal reformism. Its protagonists take the actually existing world of passionate attachments as given, and then they try to modify it—not so as to make all the attachments harmonious, a utopian rather than a reformist project, but so as to make them sufficiently compatible to coexist in peace. That seems to me something doable and worth doing: it is also, very simply, what we have to do.

DISCUSSION

Nationalism and Israel

AVISHAI MARGALIT: Richard Wollheim raised the issue of not having a criterion for being a Jew. Isaiah used to think that the quest for criteria is a Wittgensteinian obsession. We can recognize an elephant when we see one, even without having criteria for being an elephant. So why do Jews need a criterion? At least for Isaiah's generation, the question who is a Jew wasn't much of a problem.

Richard once asked, in a review, why the fact that he came from Devon should be important to him, and why the fact that he is a Jew should be a more important fact about him. Well, Richard, suppose that half of the people of Devon were to be murdered just because they were from Devon. Wouldn't it then be a terribly important fact about you that you were born in Devon? I think it would. So why is it so mysterious to you to feel solidarity with Jews? After all, they were murdered in your lifetime.

RICHARD WOLLHEIM: Actually I wasn't born in Devon at all. The issue is simply this: my mother's family came from Devon, and my father's family came from Germany.

My father's family was in origin Jewish, and I don't
know how much dilution there was by the time my
father was born. There was a great deal of intermarriage. Anyhow I can think of myself as having these
two sides. And the issue that I raised in a review was
that I cannot really understand why people always
think that I should give much more importance to one
of these sides than to the other. It has nothing to do
with the Holocaust.

In fact I have some sentiments about each, although
not very strong ones. I also have some sentiments, oddly
enough, about being German, which are more emotional to me, though I recognize them as totally absurd.
I wouldn't want them to play any part in my life what-
soever. But I think that we just find ourselves with a
whole lot of these feelings. When I was age ten or eleven
I, like Madame Bovary in her convent, was immersed
in Walter Scott. I lived like her *en plein* Walter Scott.
And this gave me the sense that I was Scottish. And this
sense of being a Scot did a great deal for me. It gave me
a sense of identity which allowed me to go through a
certain amount of persecution and bullying at school.
It gave me a sense of some dignity which I got from
Scott's heroes.

Now you may think this is something utterly different from the serious issues that we are supposed to be
talking about. I don't think it is. I think that we have all
these different identifications we make. Some we give
more weight to than others. Some are well-grounded.
Some are not well-grounded. And Isaiah, in his discussion of Disraeli and Marx, comes somewhat around to

the view that the actual factual basis of this whole thing may not be so important.

But of course, there is the question of the factual basis. And the question I raised about being a Jew, and which Avishai dismisses, is, "What really is the accepted factual basis in the case of Zionism?" It is a question which arises for me because I understand—I may be wrong in this—that by the law of return, Jewishness is a matrilineal matter. So I have no reason to associate myself with this, but nevertheless I do to some degree.

MICHAEL WALZER: I was rather taken with Richard Wollheim's discussion of anti-Semitism. I'm sure that I will caricature it as I try to reproduce it, but then he's right here to correct my understanding of what he said—which is that anti-Semites don't really hate Jews; they are the agents of some kind of free-floating aggression that just happens to light on Jews but could as easily light on other people. What's intriguing about that idea is that the whole world should therefore be grateful to the Jews for having been the object of so much aggression, which would have been focused on somebody else if we hadn't been there.

MR. WOLLHEIM: And they have been. It is true that I think that the crucial issue is what you really do think is the nature of anti-Semitism: whether you think that anti-Semitism is aggression which comes down upon Jews for some characteristics that they, Jews, actually have. Now I find that thought is preposterous. But it's held by a lot of people. Isaiah was certainly tempted by

180

it as we can see from his discussion of Jewish self-hatred. I think it's the crucial issue, because, if you really do think that Jews through something which is their Jewishness are bound to attract the hostility and the dislike and the disdain of non-Jews, then of course the world for Jews is a very different place from what you would think it to be if you think anti-Semitism corresponds to some other broader pathological pattern.

MR. WALZER: My defense of liberal nationalism and the value of statehood doesn't depend at all on an account of anti-Semitism. I believe, for example, that the French are entitled to a state even though there isn't a great deal of anti-Gallic sentiment in the world.

FRANCES KAMM [Department of Philosophy, New York University]: I received the impression from Richard Wollheim's comments that he was actually blaming the Jews for anti-Semitism on the basis that the triggering factor for anti-Semitism is *believing* one is Jewish. If we were to stop believing we were Jewish, anti-Semitism would go away. And that seemed to me to be a rather shocking statement.

My second question is for Avishai Margalit. You said that Isaiah Berlin's justification for Zionism had nothing especially to do with anti-Semitism or the history of destruction. That made it rather surprising that you referred to the history of persecution in your own justification of thinking of yourself as a Jew. You said that Berlin was concerned with the feeling of unfreedom, of not feeling at ease and not feeling at home, rather than anti-Semitism. But it seems that if all you have is a feeling of unease, and the establishment of a state is going to require a lot of energy and cause many deaths, that wouldn't be a sufficient reason for starting a state. If short people feel uncomfortable in a country where most people are taller than they, and there will be numerous murders if they try to form a state in which they're the majority, one would not think them justified. I don't know what the justification is, but it doesn't seem to me that that would be strong enough if it was Berlin's.

MR. MARGALIT: Well, I think I made it clear that Berlin did not make it an issue of justification. He believed that if your basic loyalties, like your family ties, are subjected to inspection and criticism, they might be undermined.

Actually your example of the short people is not too far from Berlin's own comparison of the Jews with hunchbacks. Some may say a hunchback is beautiful, some may try to hide it, but most are likely to be immensely ill at ease and embarrassed. This, Isaiah thought, is enough of a motivation—not a justification—for them to act. To be a Jew, or to be a Zionist, was for Isaiah more like to have certain family ties than to subscribe to a certain ideology which calls for justification. He therefore did not feel the urge to make it cohere with other beliefs he had: it was for him not so much a belief he had as a framework for his beliefs.

MR. WOLLHEIM: In response to Frances Kamm, let me make it clear that I wasn't saying anything about blame at all. Let me clarify what I was saying. If you think that anti-Semitism is a response to certain characteristics which all Jews share, then probably Zionism is a reasonable response. But, if you don't, then it seems to me that to think that being a Jew is a fundamentally important fact about oneself has its dangers because it can reinforce the belief that Jews are very different from non-Jews. Some people like to think of themselves in that way anyhow. Why not? And some Jews, those soaked in the culture, may actually be very different from non-Jews, and may be so just because they are Jews.

MARK LILLA: I'd like to take the discussion back to Isaiah Berlin for a moment. This discussion has made a little clearer to me something that we were talking about in the previous session regarding the distinction between Isaiah Berlin's attraction to the Enlightenment and Counter-Enlightenment. There are at least two ways of thinking about nationalism that I think he held. One is to treat it as a fact of life. It's a fact that people have these attachments, either because we're built that way or because of accidents of history (such as anti-Semitism). I think Michael Walzer is right to say that this view is consistent with a certain liberalism.

But there's another argument for nationalism which Berlin also makes, certainly when he talks about the Counter-Enlightenment, and that is the argument that the good life is a life with those attachments. And it's something not only that we have to cope with but that we need to cultivate and perpetuate, because liberalism, or modernity perhaps, threatens it. Now if Berlin's position really is that national attachment is just a fact of life that we have to cope with, then it seems to me that he doesn't need strong views about the perpetuation of that fact. If, for instance, through intermarriage or assimilation a people disappears, he shouldn't necessarily have strong feelings about that. On the other hand, if to live a good life is to have those attachments, then it seems to me he has to make a stronger case for perpetuating these ties, in which case he might ultimately have to sacrifice his liberalism.

MR. MARGALIT: My way of rendering it is that Isaiah started from the fact that there is this national attachment and it is vitally important to his life and to the lives of many people. But if, in the natural course of events, this attachment evaporates, then so be it. He never subscribed to the idea that Jews belong to a community of destiny. Never in their history did Jews do as well as they do in the United States. And if an American Jew decides some day to become American rather than a hyphenated American-Jew, well, so be it.

Richard mentioned a thought experiment that Isaiah used to test us with: "Suppose you have Aladdin's lamp. You rub it, and all at once all the Jews in the world turn into happy Danes. Would you rub it?" I said, "No." Isaiah thought that I had answered too promptly, that I did not take Jewish suffering seriously enough. He took Jewish suffering very seriously indeed. I don't believe Isaiah would have rubbed the lamp, but I don't know. In any case, he was not interested in any metaphysical or metahistorical idea about the Jewish people.

Also, he definitely did not believe in a triumphalist Jewish history. If anything, he believed, with Lewis Namier, that the Jews have more history of martyrdom than history.

Richard mentioned Isaiah's attitude to religion, and his description goes too far. In some schematic sense, Isaiah was anti-religious, and, by implication, anti-Jewish-religious. He vehemently hated clericalism. But, to the extent to which Jewish culture and history are inextricable from the Jewish religion, he was not alienated from it

MR. WOLLHEIM: Well, I think that Berlin's thinking on a number of subjects, one of which was religion, was the result of a number of conflicts or pressures going in, and coming from, different directions. I find myself very much in sympathy with that. I know, from my own case, that Isaiah had a very deep hostility to religion. I know it from the very deep hostility he had to the residual religious views I had when we first met in the late 1940s. Now, it is true, when confronted by the Jewish religion, he had less hostility to that than he should have had in consistency. But I think that was a point of conflict with him. I think what he really liked were very diverse societies. He liked societies in which you had lots of people of very different kinds, an enormous variety of life. I don't think he liked the idea of a society which was, in a sense, a community, at all. It did not have an intrinsic appeal to him. But I think that, in the particular context of Zionism, he felt that the whole thing might get increasingly debilitated if there wasn't some kind of adherence to a community, something or other which you therefore would want to preserve across the centuries. But I think once again he felt in conflict at that point, understandably enough.

AUDIENCE PARTICIPANT: I'd like to ask Avishai Margalit to clarify his position about Jewish identity, because I heard him say three different things. First, he objected to the proposition of any criterion, saying he was sympathetic to Berlin's proposition that a Jew is somebody who feels like a Jew. Then he suggested Jewishness is more or less like a family business, which is a rather Wittgensteinian position. Finally, he referred to the law of return, which stipulates a very precise definition. Now, whether or not we agree about the definition of the law as it is, any law would require a very precise definition to be meaningful.

MR. MARGALIT: Well, this is a direct question and it calls for a direct answer. On some level Berlin believed that the Jews are an extended family. But then, even in the case of an ordinary family it is not always all that easy to define its borders. So let me get to the real issue of the law of return, according to which every Jew is entitled to come to Israel and to get immediate, automatic, and unconditional Israeli citizenship. But who is a Jew for the purposes of this law? Five governments were toppled in Israel precisely on this issue. One famous case involved Brother Daniel, who was born to a Jewish mother but became a Carmelite monk during World War Two, and had a heroic record of saving Jews in Europe during the Holocaust. He wanted to be recognized as a Jew in the state of Israel. The Supreme Court decided that a Catholic monk cannot be considered a Jew, even if according to Jewish religious law he is. The court's decision was based on what they termed a "sociological" definition. Ben-Gurion later asked some forty prominent Jews from around the world to address the question of who is a Jew. Isaiah Berlin, who was among them, thought that this was a rather silly enterprise. But he said so in many polite words.

Isaiah once asked me what my answer would have been to Ben-Gurion's question. My answer was, and still is, that for the purposes of the law of return, a Jew is anyone defined as a Jew by the Nuremberg laws. Anyone who would have been persecuted as a Jew on the basis of the Nuremberg laws should be accepted by the state of Israel. This, I told him, is what I understand by Zionism's mission to provide the Jews with an unconditional asylum.

AUDIENCE PARTICIPANT: People occasionally suggest that the ultimate origins of Berlin's value pluralism are in his Jewish identity. Would you agree that there is a connection between his notion of pluralism and Judaism, and if so, could you explain what it is?

MR. WALZER: Those of us who are pluralists and Jews sometimes work very hard to find sources for our pluralism in Jewish history and thought—and there are possible sources, moments to recognize, texts to cite. But we are not looking to central features of the orthodox tradition when we make a move of that kind. There are astonishing statements by some of the rabbis of the talmudic period that would suggest, and have been interpreted by contemporary scholars to suggest, a pluralist, even a relativist position. But these same people had no difficulty identifying heretics. I don't think that I would base my own politics on such sources. If we want to defend pluralist positions, we should do that in the language most familiar to us—for me, that is the language of American liberalism. In Israel today, there are very good reasons to go back to the Jewish tradition and try to reinterpret it in a pluralist manner. Isaiah Berlin, I am sure, came at pluralism from another direction.

AUDIENCE PARTICIPANT: Professor Margalit's comments about the murder of people from Devon and the Nuremberg standard suggest that ultimately the justification for Zionism is just humiliation. And the feelings of not feeling at home and of not belonging are explained by anti-Semitism. But in his talk he suggested that nationalism has three independent sources: the feeling of not belonging, the feeling of not being at home, and, at least for some people, humiliation.

The feeling of not feeling at home, which is a Herderian argument that I think Berlin changed his mind from time to time about sharing, suggests that it is necessarily true that every Jew from New York to Riga to Yemen to Ethiopia felt not at home because none of these were the Jewish home. And if all of those Jews were put together in a place defined as the Jewish home, all of them would feel at home there. This is manifestly not true. People feel ill at ease for any number of reasons. And the Yemeni Jews and the Ethiopian Jews have felt ill at ease in Israel for different reasons from why they may have felt ill at ease where they were. And some American Jews might feel much more ill at ease in Israel than they do in the United States. Now if that's right, then it's really just about humiliation and anti-Semitism. But if the Herderian story is right, if Jew is just a natural kind, like German is a natural kind, like French is a natural kind, then any of those people will necessarily feel ill at ease in each others' homes. Which do you think, and which do you think Berlin thought?

MR. MARGALIT: Nobody feels at home. And everyone is a little bit shy. I once told Isaiah that not feeling at home and being socially ill at ease are among the traits that astrologists and clairvoyants use in order to play tricks on us. We all tend to believe that these traits apply precisely to ourselves—when in fact they apply to everyone. Oxford is a place in which the dominant emotion is embarrassment, and where no one feels quite at home. So I once asked, at a dinner party, who in Oxford is really "in." Isaiah Berlin's name was the only one people mentioned with confidence. (John Sparrow's name came next.) Having said that, I believe I knew what Isaiah meant when he said he did not feel at home in Oxford.

Isaiah believed, like the dark Dean of St. Paul Inge, that a nation is a bunch of people who hate their neighbors and cherish some delusions about their ancestors. Obviously a nation is a social construct and not a natural kind. But then it is far harder to change a social construct than to change a natural kind. In my kibbutz, within a few years the cows we had were changed, through artificial breeding, from Arabic cows to Dutch cows. But no one could change even the slightest social habit of that kibbutz. Isaiah believed that it does not really matter whether nationallsm is a social construct or something else: it exists all right.

Isaiah Berlin did not like what the Oxford philosopher Price used to call argybargy philosophers. You should state your position, and it should be compelling. If it is not, no argument will help. So he was not troubled by problems of coherence. I disagreed with him on that, but that's the way he felt and operated.

MR. SILVERS: Some of what we've heard seems to ignore Isaiah's own point about choice, in a remark somewhat different from the one I earlier quoted. He said, "I don't want Jews to stop living where they live. If they don't mind being a minority, that's in order. Minorities are often a valuable stimulus to a majority, a leaven, a source of information. But nobody should be forced to be a minority." We sometimes speak as if he thought that being part of a minority was necessarily unnatural. But we see here that he didn't think that this was necessarily so.

AUDIENCE PARTICIPANT: I wonder if I may suggest a simpler formulation of all of this. If this discussion were conducted a hundred years ago, very few people in this audience would have any doubt that self-determination of peoples was part of the liberal agenda of the world. And I wonder if we oughtn't to see Isaiah Berlin as a product of that view—that to a large extent his writings on the subject were an attempt, after the Second World War, to resurrect the view of liberal nationalism which was held by people in the United States and in most of Europe. Perhaps we could then look at Zionism as the very simple point that if other people were entitled to have a country and would express themselves and their freedom best there, so would Jews.

MR. MARGALIT: Had you said what you have just said a hundred and fifty years ago, you would have been right. Nationalism then sided with liberalism. Zionism, in a way, came too late—at the end of the nineteenth century, nationalism was already hijacked by the reactionary right. Zionism was therefore caught in between.

RONALD DWORKIN: Of all the fascinating things that have been said, the one that I find most alarming is Michael Walzer's idea that liberals should give up the idea that particularistic attachment can go away. If we try to defeat or overcome that attachment, you say, we are doomed to failure. Now that makes it very important to ask what kind of particularistic attachment you think inevitable. You think it inevitable that people will demand to live in a community in which they feel at home. But what does that mean?

It seems to mean, for you, a community that is governed by people like them—a community in which, if it is a democracy, their kind of people are in the majority and therefore in control. So you suggest that the best we can hope for is a liberal nationalism in which people live in a community which they control but which treats everyone, including minority groups who have different particularistic attachments, with equal concern, and which respects everyone's rights, including a minority's rights to institutions of civil society in which they can express their own, different, attachments. But of course no such liberal nationalism is possible, at least in a stable form, unless some group is prepared to accept a society in which it does not feel at home in that sense, in which it is content to enjoy the status of equal citizenship and rights without political control. If all the groups in a community insisted on feeling at home, they might agree on all the rights and interests that a liberal nationalism would provide for everyone, and yet kill one another over the single issue of which of them would be in the majority in the political territory as it's finally established.

It would make all the difference if people generally could be satisfied with the status of equal citizenship and the full protection of their rights, including their rights to express their particularistic attachments in various institutions of civil society, without also demanding that people like them be in final political control. That shift would save many lives and make many more decent lives possible. If the shift is possible for some people who are now in minorities, as your liberal nationalism assumes it is, why not for everyone or for most people? Where is it written in the human genome that this is not possible? Doesn't the history of the United States, checkered though it is, suggest that it is possible? No doubt it is a piece of great optimism to suppose that the demand for feeling at home, in your sense, will soon abate everywhere. But it would be a shame for liberals to give up their long held ambition that one day it will. Or to stop arguing and working in that direction. So long as everyone wants to live in a political community that people like him control, persuading them all to liberal nationalism won't help. Each group will want liberal nationalism, but only for itself.

MR. WALZER: Well, I did say that national self-determination can take many political forms, and I can, just possibly, imagine a post-national world in which it didn't take its present form, but some other that you would find less objectionable. I acknowledge that the kinds of passionate attachment that (as I believe) human beings require have changed over time and will continue to change. The problem that is sometimes posed for liberal political theorists by "communitarians" is whether any strong attachments could be sustained and reproduced in a society where their theories were fully realized. But I doubt that a realization of that kind is possible.

In any case, in the world in which we live there are groups like the ones that Isaiah Berlin identified with and that you presumably don't identify with. These groups exist; they sometimes fight with one another;

they engage their participants very deeply. And the immediate political problems that they pose can, I think, only be dealt with in the ways that I described: by trying to accommodate the groups in a variety of political arrangements, keeping the arrangements tentative if we can, changing them as we have to, conceding here, drawing a line there. But if you are looking for my permission to aspire to something radically different from all that . . . of course, you have my permission to aspire.

MR. DWORKIN: I want permission to aspire to it without being told that I'm bound to fail because of irrevocable human nature.

MR. WALZER: All right. I am not a world historical theorist; I don't know what is irrevocable and what isn't. But in your lifetime and mine, that project is bound to fail.

MR. WOLLHEIM: First, this phrase, "feeling at home," has taken on a life of its own, and it seems to me a very obscure idea. Certainly the conditions under which someone does feel at home vary enormously from person to person. There are people who will feel at home only in groups of like-minded people. But that is not the whole of humanity. And certainly the thinker of whom we heard only this morning that he didn't like to read the books of people he agreed with is unlikely to have felt at home largely with people with whom he was in agreement. And indeed, we know that's not so.

MR. WALZER: I think that I agree that feeling "at home" doesn't get at what made the Zionist impulse so strong. I will just mention the alternative argument put forward by the Israeli philosopher and social critic Yeshayahu Leibowitz: that the reason for Zionism is that we (the Jews) didn't want to ruled by Gentiles anymore. I suspect that such a political account of the Zionist impulse may have real value. The sense that for two thousand years we lived under alien governments, with all the vulnerabilities that suggests, and then, when opportunities appeared, we sought a government of our own. Of course, we were sometimes more, sometimes less, vulnerable; and sometimes, not always wisely (German Jews are the prime example) we certainly did feel at home in one or another diaspora setting.

FRITZ STERN [Department of History, Columbia University]: A very brief comment about the fact that, historically, liberalism was in its decline at the end of the nineteenth century just as Zionism was born. Surely Avishai would agree that liberal nationalism ought not to be taken as an abstract principle but as a state of mind. And a state of mind that Isaiah represented, that Chaim Weizmann represented, that in a very different way Tomáš Masaryk at the same time represented. And having said that and having said that they were liberal nationalists, and for all the differences between them which did exist, they were certainly of a mind against the illiberal nationalists wherever they existed.

And finally with regard to history, Isaiah's relationship to Zionism was mediated, I think, by his enormous understanding, recognition of, and admiration for the simple greatness of Chaim Weizmann himself. And since it is a fairly rare quality in historians to understand greatness, and greatness of a person and greatness of achievement, it ought to be said that this is one thing that Isaiah felt very strongly about.

MR. MARGALIT: There are two notions of liberalism running here. One is the Anglo-American notion, which has liberalism defending the rights of individuals vis-à-vis the state. The other is the central European notion, which construes liberalism in terms of the struggle of the state against the menacing power of the church. Many European liberals, therefore, were in fact believers in statism. Many Zionists too were liberals in the second sense: they wanted the state to check the power of the rabbis. They did not think much of the need to defend the rights of individuals against the state. The Anglo-American version of liberalism is in fact a latecomer to Israel. Israel is a junkyard of all the nineteenth-century ideologies; liberalism in its Anglo sense is not one of them.

THOMAS NAGEL: I believe that a central part of the difference between Michael Walzer's attitude and mine, as well as Ronald Dworkin's, toward these passionate attachments to intergenerational national traditions, is that although we all recognize that their existence, their importance and their power in limiting the political possibilities is very great and can't be denied, Michael Walzer, I think, believes that it would be unfortunate if these things ceased to have the importance for the particular communities that they have, at least in some cases, whereas others think that that wouldn't be so bad. If there was a shift in the way in which the boundaries were drawn that defined these identities, or there was assimilation here and conglomeration there and so on, we would not regard this necessarily as unfortunate.

Walzer's use of the analogy of the attachment of parents to their children, and his invocation of the creation of new Liberal man, who is imagined on the model of new Socialist man and who won't have any attachments at all, indicate that he thinks these things are intrinsically very important and valuable, and that a world in which they were weakened to the extent that they did not generate the sorts of severe political problems they now generate would be a worse world.

I actually think that his take on this general question—he spoke generally about liberal nationalism—probably reflects a particular feeling about the Jews and about Israel. And it wouldn't be reasonable or imaginable that someone who didn't have the sense that this attachment, at least, should survive indefinitely into the future, and was worth the costs, would hold the more general view that you hold.

MR. WALZER: Yes. I did think when Mark Lilla asked his question about whether this was a fact of life only, that no one really thinks it is a fact of life for whom it isn't a fact of his life. That was probably true of Isaiah Berlin. I don't aspire to a world in which people only have friends—voluntary associates, so to speak. And that is the world, compactly put, that you are describing. We are not the sort of creatures who can construct a world of meaning, each one for him or herself. That vision of human autonomy strikes me as bizarre.

I guess I believe what I've been taught in recent years about social construction: Judaism, Jewishness too, is a social construction. It took three thousand years to make it. All of us live, it seems to me, with legacies of that sort, which we acquire in and from our families, but also in and from the world our families inhabit, and which most of us, at any rate, try to pass on, sometimes in a revised version, to the next generation. I find it hard to imagine human lives that are not constituted in that way.

Now, these cultural legacies, social constructions, familial attachments can take very different political forms. They have taken different forms in the history we all know. I mean to be openminded about the forms they can take. Right now, for particular groups of people, like, say, the Palestinians, maybe the Tibetans, maybe the Kurds, political sovereignty or some strong version of autonomy may well be the necessary instrument of cultural survival. That was true, I think, for the Jews fifty years ago. But it's not an eternal truth about the state of the world. We can imagine, and it is worth trying to imagine, quite different political formations in which cultural reproduction would be possible, insofar as people want it.

I am not committed to the kinds of attachment that produce today's political troubles because I am committed to the troubles. I am more than ready to look for political arrangements in which national and religious communities would live together, where their members would have further, overlapping memberships in a wide range of organizations—trade unions, political parties, professional associations, interest groups of different sorts—and so would be bound together despite their differences. There is a lot of room for exploration and experiment in what might be called the politics of toleration or accommodation. What I can't imagine is a recognizably human way of life that does not entangle individuals in strong communities— and so require a politics like that.

ABOUT THE TYPE

The text type, Sabon, was designed by the son of a letter-painter, Jan Tschichold (1902–1974), who was jointly commissioned in 1960 by Monotype, Linotype, and Stempel to create a typeface that would yield consistent results when produced by hand-setting, or with either the Monotype or Linotype machines.

The German book designer and typographer is known for producing a wide range of designs. Tschichold's early work, considered to have revolutionized modern typography, was influenced by the avant-garde Bauhaus and characterized by bold asymmetrical sans serif faces. With his Sabon design, Tschichold demonstrates his later return to more formal and traditional typography. Sabon is based upon the roman Garamond face of Konrad Berner, who married the widow of printer Jacques Sabon. The italic Sabon is modeled after the work of Garamond's contemporary, Robert Granjon.

In Sabon, Tschichold's appreciation of classical letters melds with the practicality of consistency and readability into a sophisticated and adaptable typeface.

Sabon is a registered trademark of
Linotype-Hell AG and/or its subsidiaries

Printed and bound by R. R. Donnelley & Sons,
Harrisonburg, Virginia